I0169293

SWILL 2011

Neil Williams

Vile Fen Press

a division of Klatha Entertainment an Uldune Media company

SWILL 2011
Copyright © 2025 Neil Williams

All rights reserved. No part of this book may be reproduced or transmitted in any form or by any means, graphic, electronic, or mechanical, including photocopying, recording, taping, or by any information storage or retrieval system, without permission in writing from the publisher.

Library and Archives Canada Cataloguing in Publication

Williams, Neil, 1958-
(Jamieson-Williams, Neil, 1958-)

SWILL 2011 / Neil Williams.

ISBN 978-1-894602-28-0

   1. Science fiction--History and criticism.

2. Science fiction fans. I. Title.

Previously published as SWILL @ 30: 2011
Copyright © 2024 Neil Williams
Neil Jamieson-Williams
ISBN 978-1-894602-24-2
PN3433.5.J36 2012   809.3'8762   C2012-901693-4

Published by Vile Fen Press
an imprint of Uldune Media
504 – 635 Canterbury Street,
Woodstock, ON, Canada, L4S 8X9.
www.uldunemedia.ca

Table of Contents

Introduction: 2024

SWILL @ 30 was initiated for several reasons.

First and foremost, as a celebration of the 30th anniversary of the original SWILL (which can be found in the volume Original Swill). Reviving SWILL was to be fun. Where I could be crude, and blunt, and not politically correct, and just say what I wanted to say

This is very different from academic papers. Even more different than writing academic textbooks, where you must present the established consensus (maybe with some footnotes stating that there are competing theoretical perspectives), use inclusive language, be sensitive, and attempt not to offend (an impossibility, as there is always someone who will be offended, even if it is only regarding your punctuation choices...) and thus be bland and unthreatening and sanitised as per the present dictates of the current status quo.

The revial of SWILL was a pleasant outlet for me. Perhaps, not so pleasant for those who were offended by the return of SWILL. The actual botton line; I don't care. I really do NOT. If this little fanzine offends you, then don't read it! Simple as that. And if SWILL is so, so offensive that you are going to cause a stink with one of the several distributors of this volume; do everyone a favour and get a life!

There are plenty of things that I find offensive that are occurring in the world today, right now in 2024. Real offensive things like:

- a 55 year-old evangelical Protestant fundamentalist Christian man marrying an 11 year-old girl (in those USA states that have no minimum age for marriage) provided the man is a "Christian in good standing" and the marriage is approved by the local judge, the local Minister, and the parents of the child. The child, being a minor, gets no say in the matter. And the consummation of that marriage (child abuse/paedophilia) on the wedding night.

- Non-Muslim women being caged and doused with gasoline, then burned alive because they refuse to be willing sex slaves for their Muslim captors.
- That our corporate masters award themselves bonuses in the millions of dollars for the termination of thousands of workers.
- That you have to be careful when sitting on the park benches, to make certain that you are sitting on the edge of the seat and away from the metal spikes (to keep the homeless from sleeping on the benches at night).
- That after the pandemic, the corporations continue to increasingly gouge us with price increases (while simultaneously engaging massive layoffs and reaping record profits) and the governments just look the other way.

And I could go on...

These are real offensive actions and events that take place in the real world. So, excuse me, if I am not sensitive and make fun of your 1970s worldview, or your favourite novel, the series that influenced your life, etcetera. In the vast scheme of things, they are not important. And, neither is SWILL.

But, I will continue to publish SWILL as and when I choose to do so.

Back in 2011, the other reason for reviving SWILL was as part of a research project I was embarking on to examine science fiction fandom. SWILL was to be a place where I could float the hypotheses I was developing, request clarification from the "natives", and so on. However, my academic institution really was opposed to this research and worked to ensure that I would not receive funding for the project; even withdrawing the institution for a three year period from one of the major research funding organisations, to prevent my project from receiving funding. According to my academic institution, my research topic was the study of "freaks and weirdoes" and potentially damaging to the "brand" if the institution was associated to this research. By 2015, I had given up on the whole idea of this as a research project. However, it was originally a key factor in the revival of SWILL in 2011.

SWILL 2011 was written in an earlier period. It does not reflect the current sensibilities of the mid 2020s. There is the possibility that some individuals may be triggered. So be warned.

Unfortunately, the Print on Demand service, that is printing this volume, does not provide the option for 90+ gsm weight interior paper. This means that certain images have either been removed or reduced to greyscale for this edition.

Otherwise, please enjoy))

Neil Williams
August 2024

Original Introduction: 2012

Welcome to Swill 2011...

I am not certain as to the audiences for this volume. There will be some of you who have read Swill online and have decided that they would like a copy of Swill in nice, perfect-bound hardcopy. There will be others for whom this volume is their first encounter with Swill. I am going to pay more attention to the latter potential audience, as the former already knows what is contained within. With one brief discussion to those who have already read Swill online.

One of the questions of that audience will probably be; why are you charging for this? The brief answer is, because it costs money to produce Swill in this format. If you do not like the price charged, then, piss off. Really; there is nothing to stop you from going to the website and printing off all the pdf files yourself, three-hole punching the pages, and sticking them in a binder. You will have to pay for your own paper, ink/toner, and so on, as well as your time and labour. If you buy this volume, all of that has already been done for you. But why does it cost so much? That is because this volume is being done as print-on-demand, which is always more expensive than printing a few thousand copies of a book. There is no way about this to produce the volume in this format; most of the cover price is production cost per book, then there is a small royalty to the printer/distributor, and then a small royalty to me -- the production costs do make up the 86% of the cover price.

To those who have never read Swill online, but have
decided to buy this book anyway; what are you getting?
You are getting every single thirtieth anniversary
issue of Swill issues #8 through #12.

What is Swill?

At its core, the original Swill fanzine was a shock and
awe boot to the head at science fiction fandom.
Vicious, angry, intentionally offensive, silly,
irreverent, and obnoxious; brimming with the malicious
delight of a shock-jock gadfly screaming with feigned
anger - all sound and fury - in an effort to rattle the
comfortable status quo of the Toronto SF fan
establishment while creating the construct of some sort
of SF fan rebel or outlaw. The spirit of Swill was
that of youthful dissent in a nihilistic, smash-it-up,
shit-disturber format. While the "edge" that Swill
constructed was that of anarcho-punk nihilism the
content was a critique of SF and SF fandom.

Or so, was my recollection of what I published back in
1981. Due to the thirtieth anniversary revival of this
fanzine, copies of issues #1 and #2 were re-discovered.
Upon re-reading those issues, even by 1981 standards
the original Swill is tame. There is no shock and awe,
no Molotov cocktails, nor even any broken windows --
it's more of flaming shit bag. Nevertheless, the
original Swill was intentionally offensive, silly, and
obnoxious. And no doubt, the ultra-serious members of
fandom, those who viewed fandom as an ideal community
and FIAWOL as a sacred act, probably did perceive Swill
in 1981 much the way I described it in the paragraph
above.

The twentieth anniversary revival, as Swill Online in
2001 had as its stated goal to tease science fiction

fandom. This turned out to be insufficient motivation, and there were no updates to the website once it had been uploaded. While, I am certain that there existed segments within the SF fan population that did take offence to Swill Online (2001), I never heard about it.

Swill @ 30, the thirtieth anniversary revival had several purposes. The primary purpose was to re-introduce myself to the science fiction fan subculture (or constellation of sub-subcultures) as it had been a long time since I was a fan -- I ceased fan activity in 1985 and aside of attending (for one day only) a couple of conventions and publishing Swill Online I have had no real fan activity until 2011. Another purpose was that Swill would act as a dialogue with that segment of SF fandom known as fanzine fandom and the research project that I was initiating to study SF fandom. The whole concept of conducting research on SF fandom was a project that had been sitting around, gathering dust, for several years; the thirtieth anniversary of Swill provided the stimulus to move that project into the foreground. As well, I like producing a fanzine, I have edited about 9 different ones over the years. But the first two mentioned above were central.

And yet, Swill always has and will continue to provide a form of critique of science fiction and of science fiction fandom -- clinical and blunt and proud of its antifan heritage.

And thus, without further ado... Here's Swill 2011.

Neil Williams
2012

What's in a Name?

Multiple names are confusing. This was never a plan,
just something that happened. I am partially to blame,
or so I am told, because I chose to be a member of the
wrong religion. I am Wiccan and have initiations in
three different traditions. When my wife and I married
back in 1992, the NDP government had allowed for legal
handfasting (with a very small pool of accepted
officiants). When the Progressive Conservatives came
into power in 1995, during their first term they
quietly annulled all of the "Satanic weddings" (Wiccan
and NeoPagan handfastings) that had been permitted by
the "socialists". It wasn't until 2006 that we
discovered that the province had annulled our marriage
for religio-politiocal reasons.

So, in 1992, I became Neil Jamieson-Williams. And in
2006 I discovered that the Province of Ontario did not
recognise my marriage or my use of the surname of
Jamieson-Williams (though I could go through a legal
name change if I wanted to). The province of Ontario
did however, recognise that my wife and I were in a
common-law marriage.

Simple, I am now Neil Williams again.

Umm… Not so, simple.

My union and the Government of Canada continued to
recognise our original marriage and our surname as
Jamieson-Williams. So I was Neil Jamieson-Williams to
the federal government and Neil Williams to the
province of Ontario. Over time, this has changed as we
have had to renew documents. To the federal government
and our passports, we have to go by our legal
provincial names, so I am Neil Williams, but to the CRA

and most of the Service Canada ministries, I remain
Neil Jamieson-Williams.

This was made more murky with my former employer
placing a publication ban on me (Human Resources,
Legal, and Marketing and Strategic Branding had
determined that my research on NeoPagans, and now
science fiction fans was the "study of freaks and
weirdos" and "detrimental to the (institution) brand").
They has also reached the conclusion that that both
Neil Jamieson-Williams and Neil Williams were
"associate brands" to the academic institution and that
they had partial ownership of "this specific IP" and
could determine how and when I used "this IP"; i.e.
both versions of my name. This was done to prohibit me
from publishing or presenting at academic conferences
without permission granted by the academic institution.
This also included the publication of SWILL.

The original publication ban only restricted my use of
my academic affiliation (I was able to obtain
alternative affiliation). When that was closed off, I
self-published. This resulted in the "associated
brand" legalese. And back and forth until my academic
institution tossing the issue further up the food chain
to the Ontario College Employer Council, that agreed
that faculty names were "associate brands" of the
academic institutions they were employed by. In the
end, I used the alternative academic affiliation and
the pseudonym James William Neilson. This was short
lived as the College Employer Council warned my
academic institution that they only had partial
ownership of my name and only had the ability to
restrict me regarding academic books and articles
published in academic journals/press and papers
presented at academic conferences; not a blanket
publication ban of any and all writing. Eventually, in
the autumn of 2018, after over a decade of battle with
Human Resources, the publication and presentation ban
was lifted by my academic institution.

Of course, Human Resources only caved because this
policy was now in contravention with the new clauses in
the Collective Agreement that granted faculty limited
academic freedom, language that had been won in the
2017 strike.

So whether what I have written for SWILL is attributed
to Neil Jamieson-Williams, or Neil Williams, or James
William Neilson; it is all me -- Neil Williams, the
Lord of SWILL ;)

SWILL @ 30

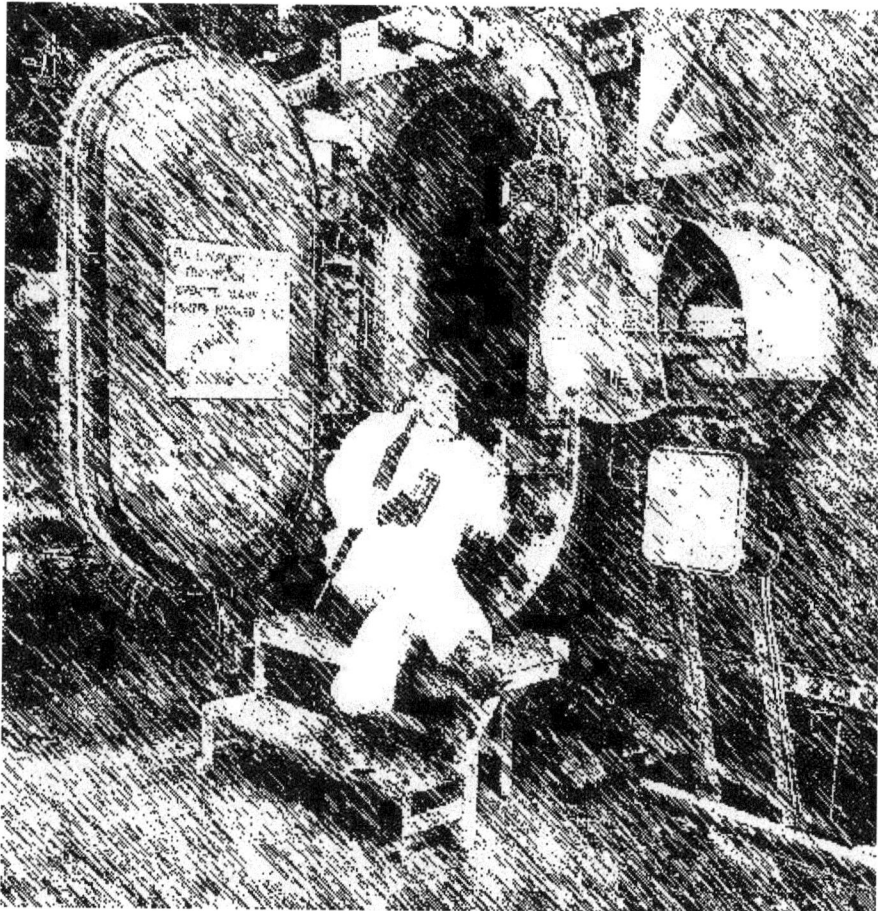

#8   Spring 2011

Table of Contents

Swill @ 30 is an evolving work...

Copyright © 1981 - 2011 VileFen Press

a division of Klatha Entertainment an Uldune Media company

All About Swill

Neil Jamieson-Williams

For a more personal recollection see *A Brief History of Swill* in Swill Online (2001).

1980 The "Maplecon Slandersheet" – a prank 'boycott' poster written by Neil Jamieson-Williams (then Williams) and Lester Rainsford. The poster was signed "OSFiC the motherfuckers" and distributed at Maplecon III in Ottawa. Some of the Maplecon organisers actually believed that the Slandersheet had been written and distributed by OSFiC (Ontario Science Fiction Club) and this created brouhaha between the two fan groups. Once Neil and Lester became aware of this – Swill was born.

1981 **Volume 1, Number 1** (February) Cover Art: Neil Jamieson-Williams (badly drawn self-caricature of Neil holding a pint of beer in his left hand and giving "the finger" with his right. Title composed of punk-style newspaper headline cut-out letters. Editorial by Neil; columns by Lester Rainsford and Andrew Hoyt; Trash the Trekkie, and a reprint of the Maplecon Slandersheet.

Volume 1, Number 2 (March) Cover Art: Neil Jamieson-Williams and Lester Rainsford – depicts three piles of shit, the one in the foreground labelled "Fandom" with lots of flies circling around it (preferred by more flies than other forms of shit). Editorial by Jamieson-Williams, subject uncertain... Lester Rainsford's column *Pissing on a Pile of Old Amazings* titled "A Gram of Brains is Worth a Pound of Shit" attacks Libertarian Party SF, Libertarian Party SF Fandom, and some of the determinist claims made by the political philosophy of the Libertarian Party. The infamous Fat Fan article (uncertain by whom; believe that the first draft was by Hoyt and then rewritten by Neil and Lester). Stephano becomes the in-house artist for Swill.

Volume 1, Number 3 (April) Cover Art: Kevin Davies – depicts Darth Vader on the toilet reading Swill. Title is also by Davies and would become the standard Swill masthead. Editorial by Jamieson-Williams on Del Rey Books advocating a boycott for the following reasons: classic reprints are overpriced, new authors are insipid, but most of all for the "self-destruct book" – Del Rey (at the time and least for the books shipped to Canada) was using a substandard adhesive for binding its paperbacks so that the pages would fall out as you read the book. *Pissing on a Pile of Old Amazings* (Rainsford) discusses the lack of original ideas in science fiction. Articles by Alicia Longspeak (Rainsford), FemFan (Hoyt), and David White (Hoyt). Stephano begins the cartoon strip *The Saga of My Fame*. Endnote editorial about the purpose of Swill – Jamieson-Williams denies that the purpose is to be nasty and obnoxious for the sake of being nasty and obnoxious – is to offer critique to both science fiction & science fiction fandom, albeit in a manner that is often nasty and obnoxious but not without humour.

Volume 1, Number 4 (May) Cover Art: Stephano – cannot recall the subject matter. Editorial by Jamieson-Williams on the disconnect between the future imagined by SF fans of the 1930s and 1940s and the world of 1981 (no World Union, no abolition of war, no fair redistribution of resources, no real conquest of space). *Pissing on a Pile of Old Amazings* (Rainsford) discussed the TTC and cycling in the Caledon Hills. Hoyt as himself bemoans the fact that the science fiction section is filled with Star Trek and Star Wars and other television and movie tie-ins but little real SF. Writing as Count Eric von Schicklegrubber (Hoyt) defends the discipline of chemistry (which appears to take second rank to physics in SF) as being as important and more relevant to the average person than physics. There are some other filler pieces, some *The Saga of My Fame* strips, and the announcement that there would be a Swill East and Swill West – Jamieson-Williams was moving to Vancouver. Arne Hanover (Rainsford) was to head up Swill East while Jamieson-Williams would edit Swill West – this didn't come to pass as May 1981 also marked the first publication of BeSwill by Stephano (BeSwill would end up becoming Swill East and Swill would be the planned Swill West).

Volume 1, Number 5 (August) Cover Art: unknown. Editorial by Jamieson-Williams that argued that the Worldcon should be called the Americancon – the convention had a mostly US focus with few international fans attending. Furthermore, at the time, only a single Worldcon had taken place in a non-English speaking country. Some reprints e.g. Rainsford's "A Gram of Brains is Worth a Pound of Shit" and other stuff. A large number were distributed at the 1981 Worldcon in Denver and a much smaller number in Vancouver.

Volume 1, Number 6 (September) Cover Art: Vaughan Fraser – shows an alien sitting on a toilet, every sheet of toilet tissue is labelled Swill. Editorial by Jamieson-Williams that discussed Maplecon III (the catalyst for Swill) and how he was pleased that they were now a proper SF convention, article by David White (Hoyt), some filler, and a reprint of the Maplecon Slandersheet. This was the final issue of Swill. This issue was distributed in Vancouver in September and in Toronto in December.

Editorial: The Spirit of Swill

Neil Jamieson-Williams

With a little trepidation, I cast my thoughts back across three decades to frame the question, "What is the spirit of Swill?"

At its core, the spirit of Swill was a shock and awe boot to the head at science fiction fandom. Vicious, angry, intentionally offensive, silly, irreverent, and obnoxious; brimming with the malicious delight of a shock-jock gadfly screaming with feigned anger – all sound and fury – in an effort to rattle the comfortable status quo of the Toronto SF fan establishment while creating the construct of some sort of SF fan rebel or outlaw. The spirit of Swill was that of youthful dissent in a nihilistic, smash-it-up, shit-disturber format.

But was it anything more than prose version of smashing windows and tossing a few Molotov cocktails? Well, yes; it was more than that. To paraphrase myself from Volume 1, Issue 3 – the spirit of Swill was to criticise both science fiction and science fiction fandom while simultaneously being humorous (albeit, a form of humour that was crass, nasty and obnoxious). While the "edge" that Swill constructed was that of anarcho-punk nihilism the content was a critique of SF and SF fandom. However, that critique tended to be sophomoric at its best and idiotic at its worst (much of the content was not intended to be taken seriously and/or written for the sole purpose of generating anger). This is hardly surprising, looking back from the vantage point of the present, I was in my early 20's and uneducated (I was a first year undergraduate who had still not been taught yet and/or had yet to learn how to discern good source material from rubbish). The spirit of Swill was critical and blunt and intentionally malicious and its target was SF and SF fandom. The odd thing is that some – not much, but some – of that criticism was and remains valid.

However, those nuggets that were and are still valid are not unique insights of Swill. They are not necessarily well thought out arguments – kind of like a vulgar and poorly written Rick Mercer rant.[1] Any valid points made in Swill have been said much better, often in more calmer and reasoned and scholarly tones.[2] Looking back over the few surviving fragments I have of Swill and Daughter of Swill, Mother of Scum as well as the content of Swill Online (2001) I have to confess, I am uncertain as to what there is to say that hasn't been discussed elsewhere and with far superior insight and reason. Is there still a purpose for Swill today, in 2011?

---

[1] Rick Mercer is a Canadian comedian and political satirist who hosts the CBC programme The Rick Mercer Report. Each episode includes a segment that is a well scripted two-minute "rant," where Mercer speaks directly into the camera about a current political or social issue.

[2] Aliens: the Anthropology of Science Fiction, 1987; The Cambridge Companion to Science Fiction, 2003 to just name a couple – an unrepresentative sample based upon a glance at my bookshelves here in my cube...

In the Editorial for Swill Online (2001)[3] I state that, "The major reason for reviving Swill is so that I can play a game, a game called teasing science fiction fandom." Well, that turned out to be insufficient motivation. While, I am certain that there existed segments within the SF fan population that did take offence to Swill Online (2001), I never heard about it – nobody sent any angry emails or even any emails, period. And that is perhaps central to the issue at hand; I am not an SF fan.

Let me qualify that, I am no longer an active member of the SF fan subculture – I ceased any real involvement back in 1985. The only "fannish" activity I have engaged in since then has been attending a couple of conventions for one day (the last one being to scout a suggested location for a documentary project I was involved on about conventions – SF conventions being one type – which didn't materialise) and the creation of Swill Online (2001). Nevertheless, although I am not a "fan", I remain a fan of SF. It is the primary genre that I read, it is one of my preferred choices in film and television, I use SF in the courses that I teach, I create hypothetical worlds and cultures for my undergraduate student assignments[4], my current research has a SF element in that it examines potential human interplanetary migration patterns, and based upon the course materials I have created, I have even started to turn my hand to writing short fiction again[5]. So, I definitely can make the claim that I am a stakeholder in regards to science fiction, but not in reference to SF fandom. It is time to remedy that.

In a specific manner, though.

I have no great desire to re-enter the SF fan community as a "fan". To use a research methodology term; I am an outside-insider who has no intention of "going native" and becoming an insider once again. To be perfectly blunt, I do not have the time to be a "fan" nor do I want my primary social network to consist of the SF "fan" community. But, it is time to re-examine SF fandom through the lens of social anthropology (and perhaps the genre simultaneously as well). And one of the tools I shall employ, in the initial stages at least, shall be Swill.

And so...

Swill is back. For how long; that is still to be determined. It will be a different Swill, perhaps a less interesting Swill; but, a Swill that has lost the in-your-face, youthful shock tactics while still retaining some of the core sprit (as well as the original focal point) of the original Swill.

Welcome to Swill @ 30. As for the spirit of this incarnation of Swill... It will be to examine SF fandom and SF in a manner that is critical and clinical and intentionally blunt. No doubt somebody will take offence...

---

[3] Not to be confused with the Head to Swill Online blogsite or the swillonline.org website.
[4] Which works better than Turnitin to reduce plagiarism.
[5] Not my strong suit, my fiction writing talents remain stronger outside of the print medium.

Pissing on a Pile of Old Amazings: Raison d'Jtre

Neil Jamieson-Williams

In the Editorial I stated, "...it is time to re-examine SF fandom through the lens of social anthropology[6] (and perhaps the genre simultaneously as well)." Well, it is certainly time that somebody in the social sciences made a study of science fiction fandom; so it might as well be me. Back in 1987, it was my intention to study science fiction fandom for my graduate work, but I was sidetracked into researching a subculture that appeared, at the time, to be more exotic.[7] And as a relatively recent ex-fan, science fiction fandom appeared rather ordinary.

Nevertheless, I almost did stick with studying science fiction fandom, for two reasons. There had been little research performed, then on science fiction fandom. Yes, there were some fan histories, but those were 100% insider accounts and histories (not actual ethnographic research), they were useful as background, foundation material, with which to design the frame for one's research. What little had been done in the social sciences tended to be very cursory overviews intended to introduce the true research topic, Scientology.[8] Thus, there was a vacuum to be filled. However, at the same time, discussions with faculty (and potential committee members) about my research topic of science fiction fandom would inevitable turn to Scientology as being a more important topic. I didn't want to do research on Scientologists, period. So, I chose to study Modern Paganism.[9]

In the decades that passed, there has been a substantial amount research conducted on science fiction fans; but, very little of this has been done within the social sciences -- and none within social anthropology. The disciplines that have performed studies on science fiction fans are literature (using historical texts and fan histories as part of the context used to ground their analysis of the fiction in), cultural studies, and folklore. Within both cultural studies and folklore

---

[6] What is called cultural anthropology in the United States and social anthropology everywhere else – the study of living human cultures and subcultures.

[7] Modern Paganism

[8] These were sociology and social psychology research articles that had really not done a proper literature review and either intentionally or inadvertently created the impression that there remained a strong link between science fiction fandom and the Church of Scientology in the 1970's and mid 1980's.

[9] As it turned out, my committee strongly suggested that I switch my topic from Modern Paganism to religious tolerance.

there is a strong post-structuralist/postmodernist theoretical framework and the primary focal points are centred on electronic media science fiction, fanfiction, and filking. All of these foci lend themselves to examining hegemonic power influences, the reinterpretation of cultural products by the cultural consumers/users, and the re-production of cultural products by the cultural consumers/users. While this can be all very interesting (and some of this research is really brilliant), it touches on only segments within the larger subculture – though some of these segments are large others are just extremely visible segments. For all of the cultural studies claimed holism, the research simply isn't -- it tends to give voice only to parts of the subculture. Although the academics who have studied filkers (SF and otherwise) generally appear to have sound ethnographic research methodologies it is probably more kind to remain silent in regards to some of the methodologies employed in cultural studies.[10]

Thus, from the perspective of the social sciences, the vacuum that existed in 1987 regarding the academic study of science fiction fandom persists to this day. It is a vacuum that I intend to address in the full course of time.

Me? Neil Jamieson-Williams, the evil editor of Swill and arch antifan? Yes, me; and why not?

I am a former fan and in my fannish days I did engage in a variety of fan activities – organising one-day conventions, participating in the organisation of multiple day conventions, filking, publishing APAs, publishing fanzines[11], and belonging to SF fan clubs. Though never a "faan", there indeed was a time when I was most definitely a "card carrying member" of the science fiction fan subculture. On top of that, I most firmly identified myself with that segment of the subculture known as literary science fiction fandom. So, I once was a fan, and now I am not. As stated in the Editorial, although I ceased fan activity, I have remained strongly connected to the science fiction genre.

As a social anthropologist and qualitative sociologist[12] – I hold advanced degrees in both fields – I have studied a fairly wide variety of subcultures within North America (in particular, Canada). I have studied software engineers, amateur and professional theatre companies, particle

---

[10] Probably the most glaring methodological offense is the use of data collected from a small sample of twenty individuals who have been interviewed for a one to two hour period; that data is then employed to make generalisations about an entire population. Although this is not a sound research methodology, I have seen this type of error occur in sociology and psychology as well.

[11] Swill is only my most notorious fan publication (next to being the editor of BCSFAzine for a year). I have published a couple of zines devoted to original fan fiction, co-edited another zine that also included Trek material as well as original fanfic, and I published a perzine devoted to space opera and the works of A. Bertram Chandler.

[12] Sociologists who use interviewing and participant observation – i.e. ethnographic research – instead of surveys to collect their data.

physicists, "open mike" musicians, Modern pagans, BBS groups (a form of palaeodigital online community), and special events (trade shows, community festivals, SF conventions, academic conferences, etc.). Adding science fiction fandom to the list would be, in my opinion, a good fit; both to my ethnographic and to my theoretical research interests.

As an ex-fan, quasi-mundane, and academic I am a kind of liminal figure here; one who is all these things simultaneously, though not. The academic role is central. I am an outside-insider; somebody who knows the norms and values, the lingo, the worldview of science fiction fandom while at the same time remaining apart, without a stake in the SF fan subculture. And the latter is actually a good thing; really, it is. It means that I no longer have any axes to grind (and I don't), though it also means that I have no incentive to try and cover over any warts that I may observe (which may not be popular with those who prefer their "truth" concealed). It does allow for a form of "objectivity"[13], a distance as well as a familiarity. It makes it possible to be clinical.

Science fiction fandom could use a critical, social science gaze, scrutinising it. It also deserves to be examined from a truly holistic approach which hasn't been done as of yet and given the degree of diversity within the subculture, may be near impossible to attain. However, if that does turn out to be the case, there are segments of the SF fan subculture that have received little attention; this could be rectified. There are many questions to be asked, but here are a few off of the top of my head…

- What are the demographics of science fiction fandom?

- Who is the average fan?

- Is SF fandom a single diverse subculture or is it an umbrella for a constellation of SF subcultures?

- With all of the involvement of cross-over groups, such as, costuming, filking, gaming, Modern Pagan, anime, etc. who is a SF fan and who is not; are there participants who are actually really fans of SF events (like conventions)?

- Is the definition of who is a SF fan a matter of individual identity and interpretation or is this defined by the subculture as a whole? If so, who determines? Does the entire subculture agree with these determinations?

---

[13] The whole Cartesian polarity of subject and object is an interesting topic of discussion; perhaps for another article…

- How do SF fans negotiate this diversity? Do they do it well, or not? Do some segments of the subculture negotiate this better than others? If so, why?

- How is SF fandom structured? Is there a structure? Are there structures, each structure organised differently?

- What does it mean to be a fan? How is this identity constructed? How is it maintained? What meaning does it give to the fan in their everyday life?

To list a few.

And that is why Swill has returned. It takes time to organise a research project (and I have yet write up a proposal to run through the ethics committee, let alone begun to develop the grant proposal) and this will form part of my pre-research research. I am reintroducing myself to the science fiction fan subculture in preparation for the initiation of a proper research project. It will be a slow process as I take in the lay of the land. I don't expect to be welcomed with open arms, either. To be frank; I don't expect to be welcomed at all. Nevertheless, it is my hope that our mutual interests will intersect and that we can both get something out of this.

And if not, well, I'm still going to do the research.

Endnote: About the Back Cover

Neil Jamieson-Williams

Well it just wouldn't be Swill if there wasn't some sort of "convention boycott" flyer. After all, it was the Maplecon 3 boycott flyer – distributed at the convention itself – that would become the source of inspiration for the original Swill. The 100 hardcopies of Swill Online that were printed all contained a boycott flyer for Ad Astra 2001 – the hardcopies were distributed at that convention. And now, Swill @ 30 asks you to support our plea to boycott SFContario 2010. *

Thank you for your support

* Temporal anomalies, chrononomic rifts, time machines, etc. not included.

SFontario

(graffiti overlay: "Boycott")

November 19 - 21, 2010

Author GoH: Michael Swanwick
Ed... G.H: Patrick and Teresa Nielsen Hayden
Fan GoH: Geri Sullivan
Filk GoH: Karen Linsley
Artist GoH: Billy Tackett
Toastmaster: Rob Sawyer

(graffiti overlay: "Tossers")

Ramada Plaza Hotel
300 Jarvis Street
Toronto, ON
M5B 2C7
(416) 977 8823

(graffiti overlay: "Vilefen Rule")

www.sfcontario.ca
con2010@sfcontario.ca

Art by Brad Foster

SWILL @ 30

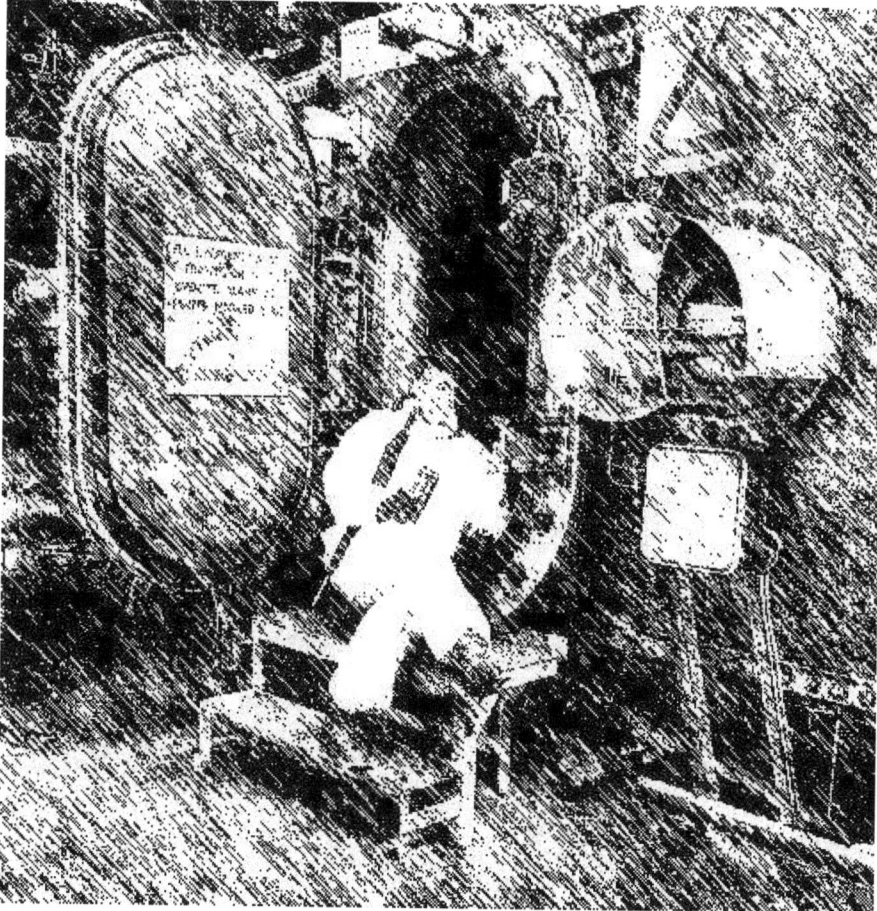

#9   Summer 2011

Table of Contents

Swill @ 30 is an evolving work that is published (roughly) quarterly.

Swill @ 30

Issue #9 Summer 2011

Copyright © 1981 - 2011 VileFen Press

a division of Klatha Entertainment an Uldune Media company

swill.uldunemedia.ca

Editorial: The Fan in the Mirror

Neil Jamieson-Williams

This issue of Swill @ 30 has evolved, unintentionally, into a theme issue; the theme being loosely constructed as what is science fiction fandom and, additionally, what is the current state of science fiction fandom? The articles in this issue will look at what academe has to say about science fiction fandom and what science fiction fans have to say about fandom. For the academics, the central issue is how they construct science fiction fandom. For fans, the central issue appears to be, is there still such a thing as science fiction fandom? I will also provide my own scholarly view of science fiction fandom as a collective in the Endnote.

However, at this juncture, I shall take a more personal reflection of what is science fiction fandom. My first definite encounter with the science fiction genre, other than occasional brushings via Saturday morning cartoons, came in the late autumn of 1969 when I received a copy of Expedition to Earth for my birthday (my parents, my mother in particular, hoped to interest me in reading fiction rather than only popular science books on palaeontology and astronomy; it worked). Over the next few months I would gobble up all the Clarke titles available – which weren't very many, maybe six, between the W.H. Smith bookstore and the local library branch in the new subdivision we resided in. I then branched out to some Asimov, bypassed Heinlein (because I had been only been recommended the juveniles which didn't interest me), discovered Larry Niven, and so on…

I recall there being a news story on CTV news about the World Science Fiction Convention being held in Toronto in 1973 and that would have been my first, albeit indirect, introduction to fandom. Now, I knew that there existed such things as science fiction conventions; I didn't actually know what a science fiction convention was and erroneously thought that the Worldcon was held every year in Toronto, but I that these events took place, far away, in the big city. The first convention I attended was the very next year (I think[1]). And I would attend convention at least once a year until 1977 when I began to attend conventions more frequently and outside of the GTA. It is from 1977 to 1985 that I actually became more involved in the fan communities

---

[1] My recollection is that it was a Star Trek convention held at the King Edward Hotel in downtown Toronto in 1974, though local fan history states that there were no conventions in the city that year. It is quite possible that I am incorrect, though I know I arrived at the convention wearing a *Starlost* t-shirt and was abducted during my first hour at the convention by some men in their twenties who carried me into a panel room and presented me to one of the panelists (Harlan Ellison, I was informed later) who went absolutely apeshit, screaming something like, "get it out of here now before I have it disemboweled." I don't think I would have been wearing a *Starlost* t-shirt if it was 1975, but maybe…

of Toronto and then Vancouver. Since 1985, I have not been involved in the fan community, period.

Until, now.

So, what is science fiction fandom? Who is a fan? Am I a fan?

I am firmly of the opinion that the science fiction fan is distinct from the consumer of the science fiction genre; all fans are genre consumers but not all genre consumers are fans. (Note: fantasy is also included here.) Furthermore, most genre consumers are not part of fandom. Most science fiction genre consumers are:

- unaware of the existence of fandom

- are uninterested in fandom

- have a disdain[2] for fandom

- are ex-fans

A science fiction fan is somebody who not only consumes the genre, but has some form of active participation with that genre and/or the fan community. The active participation (fanac) could be:

- Attending conventions, organising conventions, volunteering at conventions

- participating in genre based online forums, newsgroups, Facebook pages, twitter feeds, etc.

- writing fan fiction (original and derived[3]), fanzines, blogs, networking sites, etc.

- creating crafts, performance art forms, and visual art forms related to the genre (visual art, movies, websites, costuming, filking, theatre, etc.)

- organising the fan community

And I may have missed some… The point is, one becomes a fan by engaging in some form of semi-public and/or public activity with the genre, thus bringing you in contact with the fan

---

[2] They are aware of fandom's existence (sort of) and are contemptible of fandom; "I used to watch Voyager and the new Trek movie is brilliant, but I'm not some sort of Trekkie." Translation: I consume specific genre brands but I am not one of those freaks who dress up in costume and attend conventions. The speaker's perceptions are based on a stereotype (a generalization, usually exaggerated, of certain traits that exist within a group or subculture that are then applied to all members of that subculture) of science fiction fans.

[3] I am using this term differently to its use by cultural studies academics; I am using the term to describe: any fan created fiction that is set within a "universe" that was created by another author(s). E.g. if I write a story set within Moorcock's Jerry Cornelius multiverse it is derivative just the same as if I wrote a story set within the *StarGate:SG1* universe.

community. The degree of participation determines to what extent the individual is a fan. Many people are marginal fans a small minority are trufans; and everybody else lies somewhere along the continuum between these two poles. There are many people who may appear, to outsiders (mundanes), to be fans who really are not. For example, are the four principal male characters on the television sit-com *Big Bang Theory* actual fans?

I would say, having not read the series bible nor spent hours in analysing the dialogue, set decoration, etc, that the answer to that question is no. While all four have comic book collections, figurine collections, watch a lot of science fiction and fantasy media, play a lot of science fiction and fantasy based games, and appear to have read some science fiction and fantasy, the only "fan activity" that they participate in is that they attend ComicCon annually. Does this make them fans? In my view, no; ComicCon is a trade show. Trade shows are essentially events that act as temporary retail outlets targeted at a specific or at specific consumer audiences. Attending the Home Show does not make you a home decorating fan; neither does attending ComicCon. However, I am willing to be flexible and accept that perhaps, one could say the Big Bang Theory foursome are marginal fans – though I still think they are more heavy genre consumers than they are fans. That said, the majority of the people who regularly[4] attend fan-run conventions will tend to be actual science fiction fans.

So, am I a fan? It all depends upon the criteria used to define, fan. From my own defining criteria above; I was a genre consumer who became a fan, who ceased being a fan, yet continued to be a consumer, who is now, once more, a fan. The actual act of publishing Swill @ 30 is an act of fan activity, thus, I am a fan. Yet, I am still a form of marginal fan.[5] Fandom is certainly not a way of life, but it isn't a hobby either; my current involvement in fandom is marginal.

Yet, this is also an exploration. How does my perception of what fandom is match with fandom's perception of itself? We will see…

---

[4] Attend at least one fan-run convention per year.
[5] Though I have compounded this by agreeing to be a panelist and moderator at the Polaris convention in Toronto.

Pissing on a Pile of Old Amazings: What They Say About You...

Neil Jamieson-Williams

The "they" is academe – or to be more specific the social sciences and cultural studies – and they have had some analysis of science fiction fandom over the decades. Prior to the late 1980's the majority of academic articles in the social sciences (in particular, sociology) discussed science fiction fandom as it was in the past – that is, back in the 1940's and 1950's. This is because any discussion of science fiction as a literary genre and science fiction fans as a subculture was only a background to the central focus, Scientology. Thus, science fiction fans are depicted as predominantly male, with a strong science and/or technical background, and sometimes a "sense of wonder". Essentially, science fiction fandom is mentioned as part of the context out of which Dianetics and Scientology emerged.

Since then, science fiction fandom has been studied more in cultural studies and folklore than it has been in sociology, psychology, and anthropology. As I mentioned last issue, the focus here is on electronic media science fiction, fan fiction (with an emphasis on derived fanfic and especially slash fanfic), and filking. The majority of this research is within the postmodernist/post-structuralist paradigms[6] and feminist/queer theory perspectives within those paradigms; thus, the emphasis tends to highlight issues of hegemonic power, resistance to hegemonic influences, the reinterpretation of/re-production of cultural products by the cultural consumers/users, etc. Essentially, these are studies of electronic media science fiction fandom (or in my day, mediafen) with an emphasis on Star Trek fandom in particular. Case in point, the slang of science fiction fandom is presented in linguistics as the slang of Star Trek (Byrd, 1978) though very few of the terms reported had their origins in Star Trek fandom; they were borrowed from science fiction fandom (Southard, 1982). The work of Bacon-Smith (1992, 2000) while it does discuss science fiction fandom as a whole, does place most of the emphasis on Star Trek fandom and the fan created artefacts that emerge from Trek fandom, e.g. slash fanfic and "Mary Sue" fanfic. Although Bacon-Smith received an undergraduate degree in anthropology her

---

[6] I am being kind here; I really, really am. In an academic work I would state that neither of these supposed paradigms are yet mature enough perspectives to be called paradigms as they lack the ability to explain and predict. While they do offer some understanding and definitely offer a strong critique to other paradigms, they fail to provide an alternative framework and methodology. Of course, I am taking a social science viewpoint to the theory and methods used for disciplines that are either firmly within the humanities (Folklore) or which hover around the fence area but more on the humanities side (Cultural Studies).

doctorate is in folklore thus we cannot view her research as social science research, but within cultural studies and the humanities. Now, to be fair, other franchises are also given attention too (Star Wars, Doctor Who, Babylon 5, etc.), as are anime, filking, costuming (cosplay), fanfic, slash, and others; but the spotlight rarely falls upon the oldest segment of science fiction fandom -- the literary fan.

Now, some may say, who cares. Electronic media has won out over print; print is no longer central. This is a new century and literacy now means media literacy and the ability to use and manipulate multiple mediums. It is far more germane to examine the segments of fandom that "poach" cultural artefacts and remake them in their own worldview and for their own purposes than it is to study stodgy literary science fiction fans. Wake up and smell the coffee...

Well, I care; and these are the reasons why.

To the uber-mundane out there, a summation of the major studies of science fiction fandom over the decades would provide them with this stereotype of what a science fiction fan is. Long ago, before the mid -1960's, science fiction fans were predominantly male, nerdy, technical and science types, who read science fiction magazines and novels, some of whom were into Scientology. Since the mid-1960's fandom has changed to being predominantly female, into electronic media franchises (like Star Trek), who constantly "poach" cultural artefacts for their fanfic, filksongs, and slash fanfic, create elaborate costumes/models/replicas, and some of them are gay.[7] This would translate to the mundane as thus; they used to be math and science nerds but now they are a bunch of Trekkie freaks.

I do not think that this is an accurate representation of science fiction fandom.

The major problem that I have with these studies is that some of them are not specific in their titles – the journal article says that it is a study of science fiction fandom, but in reality it is the study of the members of the local Star Trek club in Saskatoon between 1998 and 2000. Of course, this happens all the time where the article title is more vague and punchy – even academics use hooks. The abstract will provide the general details of what the article is really about as will the article itself. However, if the abstract does not spell it out clearly that the article is only discussing Star Trek fandom, errors in perception can be made. How? Because, most people outside of the particular discipline that that particular journal is published for (very often it is the journal of an academic association/society/institute) are never going to read the article.

---

[7] For simplicity I am using the term to describe the entire homosexual, bisexual, trans community; I am old enough to recall when the term was supposed to be inclusive of male homosexuals and lesbians and bisexual persons, not just male homosexuals. While, I make some use of the Conflict paradigm (General, Marxist, Feminist) it is not my preferred theoretical perspective; nevertheless, the fact that the inclusive term was appropriated by male homosexuals as an exclusive term is an example of the patriarchy in action – thus, a nod to Feminist Conflict theory.

It may be read by academics outside of the discipline working on a similar research topic (e.g. I don't regularly trawl the linguistics, psychology, or popular culture journals).

The layperson is only going to hear about this research if it is reported by a journalist and journalists (unless they are science journalists) are not very good at translating academic studies to the average person. Here is what would usually happen. Professor X has done research on Star Trek fans that has been published in the Canadian Journal of Contemporary Studies. Professor X works at Gore University and the news of his journal article is made public in a University media release. The local paper may decide to assign the story to one of their reporters. Now a journalist is looking for a good story, something that will attract the attention of the paper's readership – best of all, get people who don't normally buy your newspaper to do so. So, the reporter is looking for an angle. If, in the study Professor X mentions that the Star Trek club has their own regular meeting place (provided by one of the members) that they use for club meetings and other functions with a footnote mentioning that the club cannot use the meeting place on Friday's as it is rented out to a local Modern Pagan group; this is something that the reporter will focus on – "Sci-Fi Satanists of Saskatoon". Journalists with more integrity will still read the media release, read the abstract, skim the article looking for good quotes and/or interesting material (as many peer reviewed articles will be very heavy in the jargon of that particular academic discipline), make a few telephone interviews, and write their piece – a piece that will tend to generalise and apply the results of Professor X's study to all science fiction fans.

Another issue is that the researcher themselves may be ignorant in some regards and thus will transmit and perpetuate that ignorance since the academic is considered an expert. There would appear to be some academics, especially postmodern/post-structuralist researchers in cultural studies, who present the literary fan as if they were an extinct ancestor to the modern mediafan. That is if they even mention history at all – history being androcentric and hegemonic bias/filter and therefore something to be avoided – many take an ahistorical approach wherein the literary fan has no existence.

As I mentioned in the last issue, this is a distortion and does not present the whole subculture. Science fiction books and magazines are still being published and purchased and read. Somebody must be buying these products and reading them and some of those genre consumers will be active as science fiction fans. The literary fan is in all probability not in decline, endangered, or extinct – just ignored. This means that scholars have not researched the entire subculture, only those parts of the subculture that fit their research interests and/or their theoretical perspectives. If your theoretical perspective is that the corporate-state hegemony creates disempowered cultural consumers who, in a better world would take back culture from hegemonic control; you are going to find more interest in the segment of fandom that appropriates branded cultural artefacts and reworks/repurposes those artefacts than you would be in the segment of fandom that creates original fan fiction. This is not unique to studies of science fiction fandom, the same thing happens in the study of other subcultures.[8] Again, a holistic research approach would attempt to study all segments of the subculture or those segments that have been underrepresented in previous studies (and actually state that this is a segment of the subculture).

At the end of the day, what académe has to say about you is that: science fiction fans are quasi-Scientologists (Spencer, 1981), gamers (Fine, 2002), or mediafen – for the most part Trekkers (Byrd, 1978; Southard, 1982; Bacon-Smith, 1992, 2000; Jindra, 1994; Frazetti, 2010), with barely any literary fen in the population.

References

Bacon-Smith, Camille
1992   Enterprising Women: Television Fandom and the Creation of Popular Myth. Philadelphia: University of Pennsylvania Press.
2000   Science Fiction Culture. Philadelphia: University of Pennsylvania Press.

Byrd, Patricia
1978   "Star Trek Lives: Trekker Slang" American Speech, Vol. 53, No. 1, pp. 52-58.

Fine, Gary Alan
2002   Shared fantasy: Role-Playing Games as Social Worlds. Chicago: University of Chicago Press.

Frazetti, Daryl
2011   The Culture of Trek Fandom: Wouldn't You Like to be a Trekkie Too? Private publication, http://independent.academia.edu/DarylFrazetti/Papers/448772/Results_Star_Trek_Fandom_Survey Accessed 10 July 2011.

Jindra, Michael
1994   "Star Trek Fandom as a Religious Phenomenon" Sociology of Religion, Vol. 55, No. 1, pp. 27-51.

Moskowitz, Sam
1988   The Immortal Storm: A History of Science Fiction Fandom. Concord, NH: Hyperion/Gibson Press.
Southard, Bruce
1982   "The Language of Science-Fiction Fan Magazines" American Speech, Vol. 57, No. 1, pp. 19-31.

Spencer, Hugh A. D.
1981   The Transcendental Engineers: The Fictional Origins of a Modern Religion. M.A. Thesis (unpublished), McMaster University, Hamilton, ON.

Warner, Harry, Jr.
2002   All Our Yesterdays: An Informal History of Science Fiction Fandom in the 1940's. Framingham, MA: NESFA Press.

---

[8] During my study of Modern Pagans there was far more literature from a Feminist Conflict theory perspective on Wicca that contained data collected from "Dianic" covens (women only) that created the impression that this was the largest segment of the Wiccan population or that this was Wicca to academic outsiders. In fact, it more reflected the theoretical and research interests of the researchers.

Flogging a Dead Trekkie:

What You Say About You

Neil Jamieson-Williams

What do you – that is science fiction fandom – have to say about you? Well, some of you – most of these people being within my age set and older – argue that fandom no longer exists. "There is no such thing as science fiction fandom…" "Fandom has lost its unity…" "Fans are now part of splinter groups…" "…everyone comes to fandom through the internet…" And various other crisis-mongering, handwringing cries of doom.

Some of this is complete rubbish and some of it is true.

"Fandom has lost its unity…" <writer is rolling on the floor convulsed in a fit of hysterical laughter> <15 BEATS> <the writer recovers and composes himself> You have got to be fucking kidding! Fan unity?! What galaxy are you from? Look, I am way, way too young to have been present for the big brouhahas of fan history (e.g. the 1939 Worldcon) but I have seen all kinds of fan wars over the years -- actually war is an inappropriate term, feud would be a better description -- all usually about pointless things. And fans are very good at holding grudges, e.g. those who are still angry about the content of the original Swill and thus have dissed Swill @ 30 based on content that was written 30 years ago. Fan unity didn't exist 30 years ago here in Canada and didn't exist back in the early decades either, according to Moskowitz and Warner, when Worldcons had attendances of less than 300 people.

Though, I am perhaps being a little semantic here, especially if the statement about "fan unity" is coupled with the statement, "Fans are now part of splinter groups…" That, there is some truth to, but only some. The argument is that once upon a time, there was a kind of unity in fandom as all fans were literary fans. That has disappeared and so fandom is splintered and disunified. Okay, maybe; maybe not. Now, depending upon which science fiction historian you subscribe to, the Golden Age runs from 1939 to 1957/1960. That means that I was either born after the Golden Age or in its final years, so I cannot speak from experience only from what I have read. But yes, in those days there were really only literary fans (comic books being a subvariety of the print medium) and the major electronic medium was radio. There was some science fiction on the radio but not enough, as far as I have researched, to spawn a distinct fandom of SF radio. And while fandom was all literary fans, some fans would choose to read one group of magazines over another, so it wasn't completely unified; each magazine was aiming its content at different segments of the audience.

When I became first involved in fandom, a shift had already taken place in science fiction with the emphasis being on novels and collections over the magazines. The magazines survived and continue to survive to this day, but their influence is nowhere near what it was in the past. With the focus being on book publishing, subgenres became more distinct, such as space opera, hard science, soft science, military, literary (new wave) to name those that existed when I was in my teens. Electronic media science fiction was on the rise due to Trek fandom and the release of Star Wars. This new segment of fandom, the media fans, was just that, a segment. In the decades since the 1970's, electronic media has grown in prominence within our society and culture; science fiction fandom has undergone the same influence.

People older than I and historians talk about the 1960's and The Counterculture; there was a time when there appeared[9] to have existed a mass Culture in our society. This was changed in the 1960's with the emergence of The Counterculture that opposed the dominant norms and values of the mass Culture. In the United States the polarisation of the 1960's is reflected in that country's "Culture War"[10] to the present day; in Canada, we had followed more of a Western European model with mass Culture and mass Counterculture fragmenting in the 1980's giving us a sluggish but fluid mainstream and a myriad of subcultures and some countercultures. The "splintering" that is bemoaned about is endemic to the culture as a whole as is the loss of "unity"; it is not a phenomenon exclusive to fandom.

The rise of the internet has increased communication between individuals. It has made communication less expensive, more available, and allows for the bypass of gatekeepers. Before the internet, telephone was the fastest form of communication and long distance charges were close to being astronomical. Post was the inexpensive means of communication used. Specialty book stores and local clubs/associations offered nexus points were new fans could meet other fans and where bulletin boards[11] provided the news of local events, like conventions. The internet does allow for that old communications system to be circumvented and for more neofen to arrive at their first convention sans any subcultural socialisation. It also can/has served to uproot/disempowered old systems of status based on being a BNF from the APA days or newsgroup days; someone who is relatively a neofan can arise to minor BNF status by running a popular and successful blog. However, this change is not unique to fandom either; it is a social phenomenon that exists within society as a whole.

---

[9] Appeared being the operative word, it wasn't as unified as it appeared and neither was The Counterculture
[10] Unfortunately, the Conservative Party of Canada is attempting to import this American cultural polarisation.
[11] Here I don't mean Bulletin Board Systems but actual physical corkboards attached to a wall.

"There is no such thing as science fiction fandom..." I think that this is absolute rubbish. To quote the Bard, this is "...a tale told by an idiot, full of sound and fury, signifying nothing." Fandom exists, but fandom has changed. Guess what, everything has changed. You cannot change the technology and not have subsequent changes in culture and in society and in subcultures (like science fiction fandom); everything is in connexion. The world has changed, fandom has changed; so, adapt to the new environment as best as you can -- and, if you so desire, you can always maintain a niche on the side that is your version of "true fandom".

Scribbling on the Bog Wall:
Letters of Comment

Neil Jamieson-Williams

As I write this, there are only two proper LoCs that have been received[12], two reviews, and one promise of a review. My comments will be in red.

From: "Taral Wayne" ~~Taral@theairy.re.ca~~

Swill? That um... I suppose you could call it a fanzine... from the 1980s. It's been a while, alright.

Hello Taral… Yes, it has been a while and all that (and it looks like you missed Swill Online in 2001). There is no supposing about Swill being a fanzine – even an antifan fanzine is still a fanzine.

ONE SWELL FOOP #3 (April 2011), the journal of diagonal relationships

Garth Spencer

I swear that one of these days I have got to do an all-reviews issue, just to catch up on the fanzines I receive in trade.

One of the most unexpected was Swill, a revival of an intentionally provocative 1980s fanzine from one of Vancouver's Surrey Contingent. I haven't decided how to respond yet (and it's been about a month).

Hi Garth… We've actually had some dialogue via personal email since Swill @ 30 was launched. I look forward to reading your review, when it comes; especially since, as I recall, you were not a big supporter of the original Swill. "The Surrey Contingent"…haven't heard that term for many years, but I did hang with that group even though I lived two blocks away from Burnaby in Vancouver.

On a side note… If you ever update your fan history and the entry on Swill, there is a slight error. While I still consider the first four issues of Swill (the ones done in Ontario) to be the best,

---

[12] The others are not LoCs but vitriolic rubbish about either the original Swill or the 20th and 30th anniversary revivals – essentially these follow a standard format of; "how dare I", followed by rantings of how unfannish/evil I am, and so on.

I do not view issue #4 to be the best issue of Swill – that honour would fall to either issue #2 or issue #3.

AURORAN LIGHTS #4 May 2011

The Fannish E-zine of the Canadian Science Fiction & Fantasy Association

Dedicated to Promoting the Prix Aurora Awards and the history of Canadian Fandom

R. Graeme Cameron

ONTARIO:

* Neil Jamieson-Williams has published a new issue of his crudzine SWILL for the first time in thirty years! Is he out to insult fandom like he used to? Worse! He's now a certified academic and wants to find out what makes us tick! Read my review of 'SWILL @ 30' later this issue.

Graeme: Like Garth we have also communicated via personal email since the Swill @ 30 launch; so, here we go in public... Studying fandom is definitely worse than insulting fandom – an insult can be spurious and unfounded whereas an academic study carries with it the aura of validity as some form of truth. Both Taral and yourself appear to have missed Swill Online – which is odd as a few months ago, prior to Swill @ 30, if you googled "swill +science fiction" the broken remains of the old Tripod site (now restored) would have been one of the top ten hits.

Swill @ 30 #7(?) April (?) 2011. A Vilefen Press Publication. – Editor: Neil Jamieson-Williams. You can read this online at < http://swill.uldunemedia.ca/ > This is one king-hell blast from the past. Swill was a deliberate crud-zine, rude, offensive, and targeted specifically at fandom, which ran six issues circa 1980/81.

Graeme: I discussed this in personal email but I might as well do so here in public and before your original numbering system becomes accepted fact. Here is my scheme. The original six issues of Swill that were published in 1981 (and only in 1981) were given volume numbers as well – okay, we first 86 the volume numbers and just focus on issue numbers. Thus, the original Swill are issues #1 through #6 (BeSwill and Daughter or Swill, Mother of Scum are – although related to Swill – distinct separate publications). The twentieth anniversary revival of Swill in 2001 – Swill Online – counts as issue #7. Swill @ 30 Spring 2011, the issue that you have reviewed is issue #8 and the next issue (the one you are reading), Summer 2011 will be issue #9.

Neil has moved on, to put it mildly. He is now "a social anthropologist and qualitative sociologist...and ... I have studied software engineers, amateur and professional theatre companies, particle physicists, open mike musicians, Modern pagans, BBS groups (a form of palaeodigital online community), and special events (trade shows, community festivals, SF conventions, academic conferences, etc.). Adding science fiction fandom to the list would be, in my opinion, a good fit; both to my ethnographic and to my theoretical research interests."

And it is a good fit. However, I just let that quote run so that I could address a sidebar issue and make a correction. Since I teach in the Faculty of Engineering (even though I am an anthropologist) I have been admonished by my colleagues for using the term "software engineers" – the vast majority of software developers are not professional engineers, they are developers of software only. Just as the MCSE I once held (for NT 4.0 for those who are interested in trivia) did not make me an actual engineer in any true definition of the term.

What sort of things would Neil Like to find out about fandom? What does it mean to be a fan? How is this identity constructed? How is it maintained? What meaning does it give to the fan in their everyday life?

In short, Neil wants to hear from you!   ...In a certain sense, Garth Spencer and I have been asking similar questions all our fannish lives. I don't know that we're any closer to coming up with answers than Neil, but perhaps we can be of some use to him in his research.

Graeme (and Garth and Lloyd) thank you for your support for the research project. Just an initial observation over the few months that Swill @ 30 has been online, it would seem that only those who remember the 1980's give a shit as to whether or not Swill @ 30 exists and of those people who do have an opinion, only those with a known and/or strong interest in the history of Canadian fandom are positive about the return in the context as a forerunner to the research project. The more faanish people who remember the original Swill hate Swill @ 30 on general principle. While it is not entirely fair for Swill @ 30 to be despised for what was written in the original Swill issues, that is just the way things are. In the true spirit of the original Swill: who the fuck cares – isn't it wonderful to be able to generate anger and offence without writing a single nasty word, simply by existing...

The above quotes seem a trifle academic in nature. Is this not a betrayal of the original purpose of SWILL? One doesn't get that impression from glancing at its pages which reflect the glory of a true crudzine, being written in pseudo-Courier typewriter font (I believe) on a 'typewriter' whose keys are so dirty the 'o' part of p, b, d, & o are filled in with black ink, rendering each page virtually unreadable.

Ah, Graeme... you have been spoiled by at least two decades of word-processing. The pudmonkey font used in Swill @ 30 is far more legible than the ancient manual typewriter I used for the "Maplecon Slandersheet" and the first two issues of Swill. However, you are correct that a revival of Swill using a clear typeface is a no-can-do.

And to top it off, the back page is an ad for SFContario covered with 'spray-painted' graffiti calling for fans to boycott the convention. This is certainly the spirit of the old SWILL, an offensive proclamation not meant to be taken seriously but thrust in your face in the hope it will annoy. Believe me, it's just a prank. Welcome back SWILL... the best of the worst...

Thanks, Graeme for the welcome back. Maybe I will win that coveted Elron this time around...

BCSFAzine

The Newsletter of the British Columbia Science Fiction Association

#456 May 2011

Felicity Walker

Swill @ 30 #7? (Neil Jamieson-Williams): Why is it good that Swill was "rude, offensive," "crass, nasty, obnoxious," and "written for the sole purpose of generating anger"?

Felicity: Why? Because it was Swill! The entire purpose of the original Swill was to give a "boot to the head" to science fiction fandom -- in particular those fans who took fandom far too seriously.

Also, I agree with Graeme that Garth and he have been asking the questions in Neil's anthropological study of fandom ("What are the demographics of science fiction fandom? Who is the average fan? Is SF fandom a single diverse subculture or is it an umbrella for a constellation of SF subcultures?" etc.) for years.

And so, if fans themselves are asking these questions, it makes it a valid area of study.

June 18, 2011

Dear Neil:

I had heard rumours of another issue of Swill here and there, and of course, when you want to find something, Google it up, and there you are. Swill @ 30 is an interesting publication, and I thought that I will treat it like any other fanzine I get, and respond to it. Perhaps that response might help you with your researches.

Of all the issues you list here, I think I have only Vol. 1, No. 3.

Lloyd, would it be possible to scan that issue and email it to me?

I might have seen your Maplecon Slandersheet because Maplecon III was my first out-of-town convention, and I might not have realized what it was. Also, the Maplecon folks at the time might have found them, and ditched them. Believe it or not, OSFS still exists, in a much smaller form, and the senior members are just that.

The concom was quite diligent in spiriting away any copies of the slandersheet they came across. Didn't know that the actual organisation still existed... Are they the people hosting CanCon?

Not sure if you are still in touch with your former fellow droogs.

Yes and no. My fellow droogs had no involvement with Swill aside of sort of cheering on the sidelines in Miriad and Nuclear Bunnies. I have had some contact, but not much, with most of my droogies over the years since we toured the convention circuit way back when with our pal Fritz.[13] The friends who where contributors on Swill (Rainsford and Hoyt) I lost touch with shortly after I my wife and I were married almost twenty years ago.

Now marking close to 35 years in SF fandom, Swill would be a necessity, if it was still possible to shock people by taking a stab at fandom itself. People would pick it up, scan it and drop it. I would say most people who go to conventions would not consider themselves part of a group we'd call fandom…that idea seems to be completely foreign to the newer people I've met who are forming their own groups and staging their own conventions.

Yes, I agree. Swill would only be shocking today for its strong "political incorrectness" – there were articles that were sexist or could be viewed as being sexist and the Maplecon Slandersheet itself contained passages that were blatantly homophobic. Of course, the entire concept behind the slandersheet and the first two issues of Swill was to shock and offend.

I have found over time the more humourless aspects and people within fandom, and I deal with them, usually, without intent, get them riled up, and then usually back away, so that others can see how foolish they really are. They scream and rant, and generally entertain most people. I try to stay constructive and positive, but a good scream and rant can be quite entertaining. Also, Yvonne and I recently wound up a career of running conventions that spanned 30 years. We'd had enough because we were tired, and our ideas didn't jibe with the majority of other people on the committee. Things have changed; so have expectations and demands of those who go, and we were slow to adjust.

Well, Swill was a prose version of intentionally riling up the humourless and over serious fans. But not as entertaining as doing it face-to-face as nobody really confronted me over Swill; they bitched behind my back, but I had to move to Vancouver to hear what a stink the fanzine had caused in Ontario.

Fandom has changed a lot over time, and yet, in some ways, hasn't changed at all. Be as blunt as you like…I don't think you'll be far wrong.

Okay, I intend to be; but in a constructive and valid manner – i.e. not just to stir things up.

Fandom, even up to a decade or so ago, saw itself as slans, a superior group, mostly because of their reading material, and a little because of self-delusion. Still, for such a literature of liberal ideas, many fans came across as dull and stodgy. (Sometimes, they still do. But, at least, they seem to realize that while fandom may be alive and still going, their part of it may be coming to an end, through simple aging and evolution of what fandom is for a younger crowd.)

---

[13] There were four of us who attended the regional con circuit and the 1980 Worldcon as droogs from A Clockwork Orange along with our pal Fritz (a dummy with a Mr. Bill face wig head) whom we would tolchock horrorshow.

Having studied a variety of subcultural groups, this is not entirely unique to fandom. The whole fans as slans concept is more unique; but, the question remains, how widespread is this at present and in what segments of the subculture does it exist in. For many literary fans, my segment of fandom when I was a fan, the changes must appear to be great as the focus has moved from the literature to the electronic media. Nevertheless, the literature persists.

Fandom could use a little navel-gazing on a professional level…the demographics of fandom are wide and varied, as are their interests. My own have covered Trek, convention attendance and operation, costuming and masquerade competitions, writing for fannish publications and steampunk. I can say I am still interested in the last two listed. There has always been someone in our outside of my interest ready to say I am not a fan (in their eyes, anyway) because I don't measure up to their arbitrary standards, or I don't share their interest, again an arbitrary standard.

I would say that fandom deserves a proper academic study and literary fandom has been largely unexplored (most of the research has been done on conventions – for the most part media fan conventions – fan fiction, and filking) to date. The demographics will probably reflect the trends within the larger culture – mass culture has become mass subcultures attended to via niche marketing and multichannel entertainment, and now, individual streamed selection.

The average fan is any person these days, anyone with an imagination who wants to explore the realm of ideas, even if the imagination is a little shallow, or the ideas are a little stale. The average fan is social to a varied extent…more and more, anyone can be a fan. The qualification is that you want to take part. Fandom, at one time, one a single subculture, but with so many different interests, movies and television shows, not to mention so many different authors and artists, we are Balkanized into a myriad of little subcultures. Over the years, Yvonne and I have tried to help out all these groups, with mixed results, but we do have friends in the Trek, Dr. Who, filk and even furry communities. While many will look down on others because of their interest (and fans seem to need to have someone to look down upon), we've tried out best to say your interest is as valid as mine, and help out with their events because we wouldn't feel like we were missing out on anything we liked, and could concentrate on the task at hand, like con suite or green room or registration.

As touched on above, we are all "balkanised" today. There is no real single mass culture and fandom is no different. How we get along with one another is something else. Fandom is not really good at this, historically – but they are not alone in having this difficulty. However, the slan notion of superiority, if it still remains would mean that fan X will tend to view their interests, say in Farscape, to be superior and thus correct and true and the interests of fan Y in Trek to be inferior.

What does it mean to be a fan? Perhaps fandom is a social support group to continually tell ourselves we aren't the geeks and nerds the media think we are, although in many cases, not all, the media is right. Fandom has embraced the derogatory terms geek and nerd, and taken them for themselves.

I think that this debate rests on accurately defining the situation and contexts. First, who is a fan and who is not. I would say the majority of the people who consume science fiction (and fantasy) as entertainment, regardless of their preferred choices of medium are not fans themselves. I know many academics and engineers who read and/or watch science fiction, but don't attend conventions and are not engaged in fandom period – these people are fans of the genre, but they are not fans. These people probably outnumber the population of fans by at least a factor of ten. Those people who have been labelled "geeks" and "nerds" do have a greater probability in being interested in science fiction and fantasy, but most of this population are not fans. There was a time, roughly fifty years ago, when most science fiction fans would have been "geeks" and "nerds" but that had already changed back when the first issue of Swill was published and has, in all probability, continued to change since 1981. However, the general public doesn't see the difference between the IT guys in the basement with all of their Star Wars paraphernalia and the science fiction fan subculture; they are one and the same from the perspective of the average person. One of the goals of my study will be to clarify this issue – of course, having the results diffuse into popular culture is another thing all together.

SFContario is the product of a slightly newer generation of con runners, but they are all people I know, who also brought in people they knew from elsewhere and other interests. Last year was a good time, and this year, it is the Canadian National Convention. So, sorry, no boycott for you! Ad Astra saw its 30th year this year, but it has changed in its focus over the years, so SFContario has moved in to cover literary SF as well.

No boycott for me! Damnit! Well, I was actually advocating the boycott of SFContario 2010 not the 2011 Canvention.

Two pages for this is fairly good, so here you are. I don't know if you intend future issues, or if this letter of comment can serve as the beginning of a conversation on fandom. Maybe I can guide you as you come back in, and get you in touch with various people, don't know what else you have in mind. If nothing else, good to see you return, and I hope you find something you might like and appreciate in fandom today. Yvonne and I have, which is why we're still around after 35 years. Let's see what your response to all this is. See you soon, I hope.

Yours,

Lloyd Penney

Well, at the outset I wasn't planning to have issues, but I changed that just hours before you emailed me your LoC. Your letter, with slight edits is in issue #9 Swill @ 30 Summer 2011. I will be attending Polaris in July; with hope, I will see you there. Neil

Endnote: What I Say About You

Neil Jamieson-Williams

And what do I have to say about you? Not too much, yet. I have been out of circulation for over two decades. Just by sticking my toes in the water I can tell that on the surface some things are the same as they ever were. As for the rest of it all; I will only know once I jump in -- which I shall do in July when I attend Polaris 25. Once I have tossed myself into full immersion environment within the subculture, albeit a temporary immersion, I will have a better idea as to what the lay of the land is.

What can I say that I haven't already said? Nothing. So, I will just repeat a few keypoints:

- Science Fiction fandom is not as unique as it thinks it is. While many fans are creative to very creative this is something that other leisure based subcultures share, e.g. little theatre.
- Science Fiction fans are not all closet Scientologists, gamers, or Trekkies.
- Science Fiction fandom is no more splintered than the rest of society is.
- Science Fiction fandom is not endangered or threatened, not even in regards to the literary fen.[14]

Beyond that, further reconnaissance is required. And so, "once more unto the breach..."

---

[14] The fact that there is a brand new literary fan convention in Toronto, SFContario, would lend support to the hypothesis that literary science fiction fandom is quite alive. I would also offer another hypothesis, that literary science fiction fandom rather than being on the wane, may actually be a kind of silent, or quiet, majority within fandom.

IMPORTANT BADGE INFORMATION: Your badge is your proof of membership, and is required to be worn and visible at all times. Please note, in response to many of our members expressing problems or concerns with the print on their badges, POLARIS changed the format of its badges. While we will have samples for purchase – and there will be a limited number of clips available – we remind you to bring a lanyard to hold your badge during your time at the convention.

THRASH ALL TREKKIES

PROGRESS REPORT

POLARIS 25
COME. CELEBRATE. IMAGINATION.

JULY 15-17, 2011

Sheraton Parkway Toronto North Hotel

www.tcon.ca

BRANDON SANDERSON

DETAILS!

CELEBRATING OUR 25TH ANNIVERSARY!

Register and Pay Online at:
www.tcon.ca/polaris

TCON Promotional Society
P.O. Box 7097, Station A
Toronto, ON M5W 1X7
Canada

mediæn sux

Anarchy @ TCON

vilefen Rule

SWIFF

@ 30

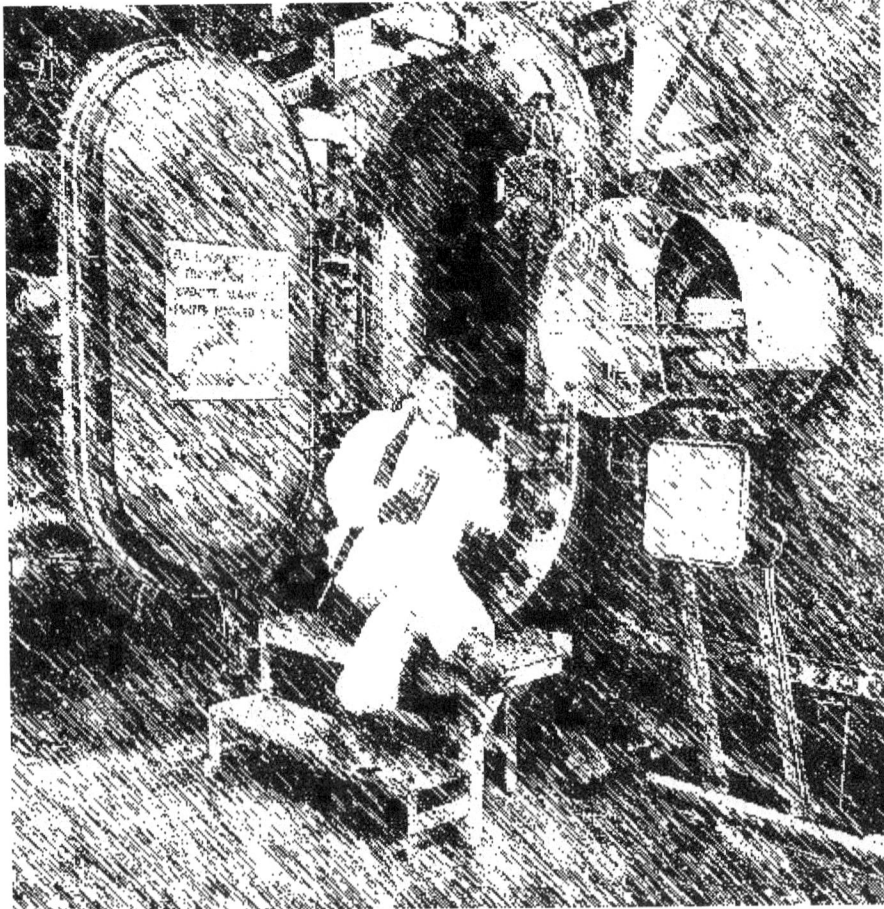

#10   Autumn 2011

Table of Contents

Swill @ 30 is published quarterly (Spring, Summer, Autumn, and Winter) along with an annual every February – in other words, five times per year.

Swill @ 30

Issue #10 Autumn 2011

Copyright © 1981 - 2011 VileFen Press

a division of Klatha Entertainment an Uldune Media company

swill.uldunemedia.ca

Editorial: A Slightly Dysfunctional Time Machine

Neil Jamieson-Williams

It's a funny thing, memory -- it is neither as clear nor as correct as we often think it is. Especially when we are engaged in the act of self-archaeology; the excavation of our remembered experiences. At times, that which we recall as being deposited in a particular stratum can be in error. In absence of corroborating evidence, such as written documents and other records that bear a precise stamp of time, there is uncertainty. And yet, those pieces of our past that possess a strong emotive quality; these carry the pure essence of truth, even though they may lack precision in sequence and detail.

I remember fondly the first SF convention that I attended, but it is now quite clear that what I stated in my editorial in the last issue was in error. My first convention did not take place in 1974 and it was not a Star Trek convention; however, I did attend FanFair III in 1975 which the Toronto fan historians appear to be split on as to whether or not FanFair III classifies as a SF convention, though they do agree that it was not a Star Trek convention (though the convention did have a strong media -- mostly Star Trek -- component to it). Nevertheless, FanFair III was my first convention.

The errors in recollection here are minor. I was out one year and the fact that I preceived the convention to be devoted mostly to Star Trek probably has more to do with this being the recollected memory through the eyes of a teenage neofan and how I, at that time, classified what I experienced. Errors in recollection become more important with the next memory site -- the inciting event that would create the original Swill; the Maplecon Slandersheet.

Here the central question is: which Maplecon did the Slandersheet appear at? To be perfectly honest, I don't know for certain. I am certain of one thing, it was not Maplecon 1 in 1978. I used to be certain that it was Maplecon 3 in 1980, but I am no longer certain of that. Here is what I am certain of:

- Swill began in February of 1981 and had a reprint of the Slandersheet as its back cover.

- I only attended one Maplecon convention.

- Lester Rainsford and Andrew Hoyt attended only one Maplecon convention.

- The Maplecon convention that I attended was one of the first that we entered the droogs in as a group costume.

- The Maplecon that Lester and Andrew attended was the same Maplecon that the droogs won best group costume at.

- Noreascon 2 (Labour Day weekend 1980) was the last convention that we did the droogs at as floor costumes.

- I was not accepted into university for Fall of 1980 because two credits from my original high school in Brampton had not been transferred as university stream credits.

- I returned home to suburbia to complete these credits during the Fall of 1980.

Putting this all together...(here is where a copy of Swill #1 would be very useful)

In all probability, Lester and Andrew, as well as the droogs (including me) attended Maplecon 2. Here is why. Both parties have a recollection of there being two to three overweight Trekkies at the convention. They were in TOS costume and running around on the convention floor of the hotel shooting each other and others with phaser guns (one version has the weapons being phaser water pistols).

Headnote[1]: Maplecon   The Droogs

We had just finished what we thought was our only judging for best group costume. During the performance, we had beat Fritz so thoroughly that he had come apart. We were in the hall outside the judging room re-assembling Fritz when two overweight Trekkies came around the corner and pointed phasers at us. The tallest droog stared them down and shook his head, "No." The Trekkies got the message and turned and ran back the way they came. About the same time we were told that the judges wanted to see us perform a second time...

---

[1] A headnote is a mental fieldnote. For every written fieldnote there are a score of headnotes that connect to it. In some ways, headnotes are as important as fieldnotes; written fieldnotes serving as jogs for the anthropologist's memory.

There were two chairs and an end table at each end of the hall that overlooked the ballroom. Andrew and I were sitting there. Then we noticed three very fat Trekkies running down the hall toward us. Andrew and I began to speculate as to whether or not they would be able to negotiate the turn and, if not, which one of us would be crushed to death under 900 pounds of Trekkie...[2]

I think that this is sufficient enough to support the position that the droogs, Lester, and Andrew were in all probability attending the same Maplecon convention.

So, the droogs and the Slandersheet took place in the Fall of 1979 at Maplecon 2. The droogs would attend many other conventions between Maplecon 2 and Noreascon 2 in 1980. So, the Maplecon Slandersheet had been written in my apartment in Toronto just days before the convention in 1979 (this makes sense as Lester and I lived within walking distance from each other at this time). The reason why I didn't hear any brouhaha from the BNFs of Toronto is because 1) I wasn't part of that inner circle and 2) after Noreascon 2 I moved back to the burbs to finish off these two high school credits. The only fan activity I was involved in during the Fall of 1980 was that I would come down to the monthly fan party hosted by one of the Toronto BNFs and it was there that I heard about the stir that the Slandersheet had caused. When I moved back to Toronto (albeit Downsview) in January of 1981 and told Lester, the idea for Swill was born. Swill #1 was published just in time for the February fan party; I brought about 10 to 15 copies of Swill to give away and I also printed up about fifty copies of the Slandersheet to hand out.

Or so I think.

It is the best reconstruction of events that I can create that fits with what I recall, what others have recalled, and the only supporting document that I have at hand (the date that I officially completed grade 13). A copy of Miriad #2 (which I think has a picture of me in droog costume in it) which was published in September 1980 would add further support as would a copy of Swill #1 as it would contain the Maplecon boycott flyer.

But memory is a fickle thing. This is a concern as my headnotes, based on my past activity as a fan, are a starting point for this research project. The question is; will my memory pass a CRC (cyclical redundancy check)?

---

[2] This incident would be the germ for the infamous "Fat Fan" article that ran in Swill #2.

Pissing on a Pile of Old Amazings: Notes and Queries on a SF Convention

Neil Jamieson-Williams

There is a book that used to be indispensible for social anthropologists planning their fieldwork entitled Notes and Queries on Anthropology that was published by the Royal Anthropological Institute.[3] The RAI ceased publication of this book in the 1960's as theoretical perspectives had changed. Notes and Queries fit well with the paradigm (or theoretical perspective) of Structural-Functionalism which dominated British anthropology for most of the early to middle 20th century. In using the book, the anthropologist would classify the culture they were studying under headings such as Social Structure, Ritual and Belief, Social Life of the Individual, etc. There would be subheadings under each of the headings. Within the Structural-Functionalist paradigm, the anthropologist would identify and analyse the social structures of a culture and then examine how those structures function (or dysfunction) for the culture as a whole and for the individuals within that culture. As I have already said, nobody really works within this paradigm today; but, sometimes it remains a useful "jumping off" point. That is, it does not hurt to use this approach for categorising and classification -- so long as you remain aware that these categories and classifications are arbitrary at their worst and social constructions at their best (in other words, so long as you remain aware that you created them in the first place).

In terms of structure, a science fiction convention is really no different than any other annual public special event. The overall structure of a three-day science fiction convention is essentially the same as that of a three-day academic conference; some form of programming during the day (workshops, panels, lectures, presentations, sessions), some formal events in the evening (screenings, pub crawl, keynote speaker, dance, concert), and a culminating event -- that usually takes place on the evening of the second day (masquerade, dance, banquet, awards ceremony, keynote address). Informal programming will be organised by the participants to the event -- the attendees of the conference or convention -- that take the form of room parties, pub crawls, sing-a-longs, karaoke, etc. The structure of these types special event is easy to determine; most have a

---

[3] I am a Fellow of the RAI.

printed programme book that is provided to the attendees and some special events retain the programme books of previous years on their website.

The primary function of an annual public special event is that it brings together a large group of diverse people who also share a common interest or interests together, face-to-face, for a period of a few days. It creates a kind of temporary community. For special events that have been running continuously for ten or more years, the event itself creates a temporally cyclical face-to-face community. There will be people who attend the event every year, who only really interact with the friends that they know through the event, at the event itself. However, there will always be people for who this event is their very first one attended, or the first event devoted to this specific interest, or the first event outside of their locality/region -- in other words, people who arrive at the event as strangers. Some events deal with strangers and newbies better than others. Academic conferences are not the best with this, there may be a "mixer event" the first evening of the conference (or often the evening before the conference as those attending from far away will tend to arrive the night before the conference starts) to act as an icebreaker. However, the general attitude is that you are a grown up academic, you will be able to negotiate this yourself. Newbies are often unconsidered because they are supposedly taken care of. A first year graduate student or senior undergraduate student will usually have attended because the professor who is their supervisor/advisor has suggested that they attend and that usually means that that professor is also in attendance; so it is assumed that there is a responsible academic present to instruct the newbies. Some of the larger conferences have programming and sessions specifically for undergraduate attendees -- which sort of acts as a "daycare" or "kiddie table". Science fiction conventions deal with strangers and newbies quite well, given that there is no assumption that there is somebody acting as "the adult" for these neos. Thus, it is seen as an individual choice -- the neo makes their own decision as to whether or not they attend the panels and/or events that are there to assist the process of enculturating them into a generalised version of the science fiction fan subculture.

My first impression, after attending Polaris 25, is that -- from a structure and function POV -- things haven't really changed very much. Does that mean everything is the same? No, it does not.

There is a greater age range than in the past, even for a media SF convention. Or, perhaps it would be more correct to say that the under 19's are staying on into the evening and night. In the past, this crowd would either vanish to the movie and gaming rooms after the regular programming ended around 7 - 8 PM or simply go home. Today, they are still about until the last panel ends (which in the case of Polaris is at 2:00 AM). With SF cons being not entirely an adult event, this means that the underage attendees have to be accommodated with late, late programming, an all-ages masquerade, and no punk or heavy metal music played at the dances (unless the song has absolutely no swear words).[4]

There variety in type of mediafen has increased greatly. Of course, time has passed and there have been many successful SF franchises since the year 1986 -- back then, there was just Star Trek (TOS and animated), Star Wars, Battlestar Galactica, and Doctor Who. It was a time period when all mediafen could be lumped together as one group (note: the same could be said of the literary fen of the same time period). So, the "fragmenting" that everybody is talking about is real; this is prominent in the diversity among mediafen as everybody has their favourite television series and some people are exclusive fans of that particular series -- I am not saying that these fans will not watch any other SF series, but, they will only purchase items related to their series. This means that there are now more distinct segments within media fandom and that makes the task before any anthropologist more daunting; the effort to construct a holistic account of the subculture becomes more difficult. That said, the trend was already present in the early 1980's with the small, but noticeable divide between Star Trek and Star Wars fans; with more SF television series having been produced since then, it is a logical extrapolation that this segmentation would occur within mediafen. Yet, a loose unity exists overall -- everyone has a common interest in SF & F media.

One of the other differences from the past is that Polaris, a SF media convention, has made accommodations to the literary fan. There is some programming that is focused on the print medium, not a lot, but some. In a way, this is kind of a role reversal as I recall the days when at a literary convention there would be a few programming items put on to accommodate the mediafen.

Anime and costuming and cosplay are more separate, but allied fandoms, than they were in the past. As a side note, the term cosplay is not a term I recall from my old fan days. The definitions I have gleaned are that it is form of costumed performance art that emerged within anime fandom and spread to SF fandom. If I have the term defined correctly, then what we did, way back, as A Clockwork Orange droogs was more cosplay than costuming. Anime also has their own conventions, as does costuming, as does filk. Which brings me to another difference from the past -- a decline in filking, at least at Polaris. There did not appear to be an official late, late night filk room organised (I don't know if there was an unofficial one) and the official filking

---

[4] I am making the assumption that the same care is taking place in regards to Rap family of music subgenres...

in the programme was in the early evening. There were not a lot of people involved and most appeared to be 40 plus years of age and singing filks that drew upon the Star Trek franchise only. Perhaps this is unique to the Polaris convention, or maybe it is a trend within mediafen in general (though it could be across the board -- I'll check that out at SFContario).

As a medium sized mediafen convention, Polaris was what I expected. There was the focus on seeing the stars, and lining up for autograph sessions, purchasing official merchandise, and all that which goes with a mediafan convention. However, the overall atmosphere was fannish. Different, but fannish.

Flogging a Dead Trekkie:

Definitional Parameters...

Neil Jamieson-Williams

And now for something completely different... Something so very unSwill-like... Something that flies in the face of the original spirit of Swill... An admission of error and a retraction. The error? Native bias.

Back when I was a fan, I was a literary fan. I tended to see SF fandom through that lens. However, I also liked media SF and had friends who were media fans. So, even though I am examining SF fandom as an academic, I have to be wary of my native bias.

I am an outside-insider. I am a former insider who is now outside of the group. That means that I am still aware of a lot of the inner knowledge of the group, how it operates, its slang, etc. However, that insider knowledge is not current, is dated, and may no longer be valid. I am also, as being outside, not in the loop as to the burning issues of the day – though some of the old issues remain within some segments of the group population. So, although I am studying this group with open eyes and a clinical view; I retain some blinders from my days as an insider. One particular blinder has to do with the definition of "who is a fan?"

I have to retract, or at least be more inclusive, than I was in the previous issue. Some of my readers will not agree with me, but there is a strong precedent – outside of SF fandom – that I will be drawing upon. For the anthropologist, when it comes to defining identity (which is what the question is all about) it is a situation where the majority does rule. How the majority of a culture, or subculture, define their identity is the definition we go with. It is the definition of identity that is representative of the culture. Gone are the days when the anthropologist themself defined the identity of the culture, or when they accepted the definition of the elite group within that culture. This means that different segments within a culture can have different definitions of identity – often this is central to what makes them a different segment. This is the situation within SF fandom, like it or not.

Before I go further, I want to provide an example from my earlier research on a different subculture that is very applicable to the situation within SF fandom. That subculture is Modern

Paganism, with particular emphasis on the Wiccan religion. There are two major groupings within the Wiccan religion; BTW (British Traditional Wicca) and Eclectic Wicca. The term BTW is a term created by British Traditional Wiccans while the term Eclectic Wicca is a term created by academics. Since, at least, the 1960 s Wiccans have been debating among themselves, often vehemently, the question of, "who is a Wiccan?" The earliest Wiccans, BTW, claim that only those persons who have been initiated into one of their traditions (religious orders) can call themselves Wiccan. The later Eclectic Wiccans state that their traditions are also Wiccan – they include BTW into their definition of Wicca. Even though BTW are the founding traditions within the Wiccan religion, Eclectic Wiccans now far outnumber them. It is Eclectic Wicca that has the most influence and control within the Wiccan religion, more or less; it gets a little muddy and complex, so we will leave it at that for the purposes of this column.

Does any of this sound familiar?

The retraction I would like to make centres on the following comment I made in the last issue regarding the four male principles in the television series The Big Bang Theory. I said:

> While all four have comic book collections, figurine collections, watch a lot of science fiction and fantasy media, play a lot of science fiction and fantasy based games, and appear to have read some science fiction and fantasy, the only "fan activity" that they participate in is that they attend ComicCon annually. Does this make them fans? In my view, no; ComicCon is a trade show. Trade shows are essentially events that act as temporary retail outlets targeted at a specific or at specific consumer audiences. Attending the Home Show does not make you a home decorating fan; neither does attending ComicCon. However, I am willing to be flexible and accept that perhaps, one could say the Big Bang Theory foursome are marginal fans – though I still think they are more heavy genre consumers than they are fans.

At Polaris, I had a lengthy discussion on this subject with a person on the concom. They related this story about an event he attended in New York City. I cannot recall the actual event, but it was a last minute event, and one that required you to wait in line all night – at least – for admission.

Headnote: Polaris 25   The NYC Event

*The line was huge, it went around the building and further.
Some people had arrived prepared with chairs and sleeping
bags and other gear. Some had not. There was an excitement
in the air. We felt bonded on some level. Those in line
negotiated place-holders and people started moving up and
down the line talking, sharing. Some of us began to call it
LineCon...*

Therefore, I would like to retract and reformulate some of my comments from Issue #9 on the subject of heavy genre consumers vs fans. As an anthropologist studying fandom it is not my role to answer the question "who is a fan?" anymore than it was my role to determine "who is a Wiccan?" when I was researching Modern Pagans. It is the population under study that actually makes those decisions; my role is to observe and describe how the subculture defines itself and illustrate that there are multiple definitions in operation within the subculture. As it is within Modern Paganism, there are multiple definitions of identity within the SF fan subculture. These definitions of identity are layered and many of the boundaries are blurred. I will start with the most inclusive and move to the most exclusive. The terminology I am using is provisional and open to further discussion.

Genre consumers: These individuals consume science fiction and fantasy content in a variety of mediums from print to television to gaming, etc. They also have an interest in science fiction and fantasy collectables. They may attend conventions like Comic Con or Sci-Fi Fan Expo. People within this group do not identify themselves as SF fans.

Fans: These individuals consume science fiction and fantasy content in a variety of mediums from print to television to gaming, etc. They also have an interest in science fiction and fantasy collectables. They regularly attend conventions like Comic Con or Sci-Fi Fan Expo. People within this group identify themselves as SF fans; the male foursome from The Big Bang Theory would fit in this category.

Active Fans: These individuals consume science fiction and fantasy content in a variety of mediums from print to television to gaming, etc. They may also have an interest in science fiction and fantasy collectables. They may attend or they may regularly attend fan-run conventions like Polaris and Ad Astra -- they may also attend conventions like Comic Con or Sci-Fi Fan Expo. They may participate the organisation and running of fan-run conventions.

They may participate in genre based online forums, newsgroups, Facebook pages, Twitter feeds, etc. They may participate in writing fan fiction, blogs, networking sites, and fanzines. They may create crafts, visual art forms, and performance art forms related to the genre. They may network and organise within the fan community. People within this group identify themselves as SF fans. Most literary fans and media fans would fall into this category.

Traditional Fans: These individuals consume science fiction and fantasy content with an emphasis upon the print medium, though they may consume science fiction and fantasy content from other mediums. They may also have an interest in science fiction and fantasy collectables. They may participate in genre based online forums, newsgroups, Facebook pages, Twitter feeds, etc. They may participate in writing fan fiction, blogs, networking sites, and fanzines. They may create crafts, visual art forms, and performance art forms related to the genre. They may network and organise within the fan community. They rarely attend SF conventions and if they do, they only attend fan-run conventions. People within this group identify themselves as SF fans.

All fans are genre consumers but not all genre consumers are fans; all active fans are fans, but not all fans are active fans; all traditional fans are active fans, but not all active fans are traditional fans. All traditional fans consider themselves to be true fans and all other categories to be fake fans or genre consumers. All active fans consider themselves to be true fans and include traditional fans as being true fans, while fans are viewed as being fake fans or genre consumers. Fans would view both active fans and traditional fans as being fans and may tend to view genre consumers as also being fans -- they have no notion of the concept of a true fan.

Uncle Swill's Guide to Creating Your Own Fanzine

Preamble:

Uncle Swill knows what some of you are thinking... Fanzines are so last century. That's how fans used to communicate before there was email, Internet, blogs, and Facebook. Why would you even want create a fanzine today? Well, why would you want to create a blog? At the core, the reasons are pretty much the same.

A web log (blog) is a type of website maintained by an individual (or sometimes a group) that contain commentary on a particular subject, descriptions of events, and other material -- usually a blog contains text, images, and links to other sites. Most, but not all, are emergent in that they are interactive; visitors are allowed to leave comments about blog content, comments left by other visitors, and instant message other visitors. In this respect, a blog can be seen as being atemporal.

A fanzine is a type of publication maintained by an individual (or sometimes a group) that contain commentary on a particular subject, descriptions of events, and other material -- usually a fanzine contains text, images, and LoC (Letters of Comment). LoCs allow for a form of emergent content to take place; however, at a far slower pace than what can occur within a blog. Most fanzines, but not all, tend to be static and sequential; each issue of a fanzine is a unique entity, followed by another issue that is itself a separate entity -- collectively, each of those issues combined creates the whole that is the fanzine. It is this that distinguishes the fanzine from the blog as a unique contemporary literary form.

So, here is the big question; Uncle Swill asks, "Do you want to do the same thing that over 150 million people are doing worldwide or do you want to do something different, something that only several thousand people are engaged in?" If you answered that you wanted to do something different, fanzine publication could be for you.

Getting Started

So, what's it going to be, then... What do you want to write about? Only you know that answer. Perhaps you have a favourite SF television series, a favourite series of novels, an opinion on the casting of Actor X as the protagonist in the film adaptation of Novel Z, a grudge over something that happened at last year's convention, some original fiction/poetry you have written, an oped piece on the Hugo Award nomination process, a slice of life personal reflection, etc. It is all up to you; but, if you are going to publish a fanzine (or do a blog), you will have to write some content.

And in this you are completely and totally free. You can write a fanzine that is essentially a public diary or stream of consciousness segments, or it can have a specific topic range (e.g. the works of Larry Niven, or 1990's British space opera), or it can take a particular stance politically (with a narrow focus as in issue X within Canadian fandom or a wider focus as in issue Y within

SF fandom and its connexion to the Occupy Movement or just a general political stance that can be linked to fandom, to the works of particular authors, and events in the world), or certain themes that you devise (a cycberpunk issue, a Gor issue, etc.), etc. The doors are wide open.

You are going to have to give your fanzine a name. It would probably be good to take a browse of Bill Burns' site **http://efanzines.com** just to make certain that you don't choose the same name as a major fanzine of forty years ago. Once you have your title, you should come up with your fanzine's "masthead" -- the font and orientation that the fanzine title will appear in on your front cover.

Structure

The general structure for a fanzine is this:

Front Cover (usually has artwork, but not mandatory)

Table of Contents (optional)

Content (editorial, articles, humour, artwork/comics, poetry...)

LoCs (optional)

Back Cover (usually has artwork, but again, not mandatory)

Contact Information (email usually, or postal address) -- somewhere within the fanzine (your choice)

This is just a general structure of what would be in a typical fanzine. However, take or toss whatever feels right to you in this structure. The freedom to innovate is yours.

Publication

Once you have written/edited your fanzine, designed the layout and the artwork, and all that stuff; it is time to publish. This is easier than ever. In all probability, the software that has been used for editing, composition, and layout of your fanzine will allow you to save the final product as a pdf file (if it doesn't, there exists freeware converters that can be downloaded). Once you have your fanzine as a pdf you should contact Bill Burns at **billb@efanzines.com** about hosting your fanzine on the efanzines.com website (it's free). And voila, you have published your first fanzine.

Hybrids

Just because you have published a fanzine, doesn't mean that your fanzine cannot have a website, a blog, or a Facebook presence -- many do. If that suits you and how you view your fanzine; then do it. A more low-tech hybrid are those fanzines that publish one or more issues a year that are only available in the print medium (the other issues being available online). There are also very few fanzines that occasionally publish an issue in another medium, e.g. an all audio issue as a podcast. Finally, while not a hybrid form, there are a few people out there who are so committed to the print medium that their fanzines are only available as printed on paper and sent via post.

So kids, that's how you create your very own fanzine. Fanzine publication is a contemporary hobby that is a part of many subcultures -- from sports fans to comic book fans, from punk rockers to wargamers -- which has a long history within science fiction fandom. Just remember to also have **fun**.

Swill @ 30

swill.uldunemedia.ca

Scribbling on the Bog Wall
Letters of Comment

Neil Jamieson-Williams

As I write this, there are three long LoCs that have been received. My comments are in red.

Re: Swill @ 30 #9 Summer 2011 now available

From: "Taral Wayne"

Date: Tue, July 19, 2011 4:05 pm

To: swill@uldunemedia.ca

Having a little trouble sending. This make the third attempt.

Hi Taral. I did receive all three emails, though the second attempt was only partial. I guess that my mail server didn't like your mail server that day...

That has got to be the most off-putting and difficult to read type font ever. Except for maybe this, or perhaps this. But, yes, I got the joke. There were even one or two fanzines whose stencils were worse.

More mail server idiosyncrasies... I didn't receive your examples in the fonts you used, but I am very well aware that it is a difficult font. But, that is the whole point. The font is more readable if you enlarge it, one of the reasons for publishing Swill as a pdf. The font is set in stone for what will go up on the website; however, for the select few (such as yourself) who receive Swill via email, as of this issue you will receive it in both the real Swill version and Old Fart version -- your choice as to which version you choose to read.

The issues you discuss are far from new. SF fans were questioning their identity and where fandom was going way back when I first got involved, and the tendency has grown. So, you may not be shocking people as much as you think. Much of my own fanwriting of late has been an attempt to try to understand traditional fandoms real place in the universe, both as in insignificant amount of signal noise and as something quite distinct from 100,000 people at San Diego Comics Con stampeding to buy the latest Star Wars action figure or Marvel comic adaptation of a movie adapting a Marvel comic book. There are no simple answers, as there might be for "who is a Presbyterian" or "what is the Nazi Party," unfortunately. Even the most hidebound old-timer in fandom probably enjoyed episodes of Star Trek. What he objected to was the Trekkie who had no other experience with science fiction other than Kirk, Spock and McCoy, and mistakenly believed the TV show was the origin of everything from character humour to transporter beams.

I tackle the issue of "who is a fan?" again in the Flogging a Dead Trekkie column. You probably won't like what I have to say, though. Identity questioning has certainly been around for some time in fandom and I agree it is nothing new. I am approaching it from the position of an Outside –Insider (a former insider looking at fandom with an outsider's POV) and therefore I have to strive to be inclusive as well as rational, logical, and fair. I did not think my raising the question would be shocking at all; this incarnation of Swill does not seek to shock and disturb, though it will not pull back from making observations that some may find disturbing.

I, myself, am quite partial to various SF toys and model spaceships. If it didn't cost as much as a new Ford Focus, I've love to have all of Star Trek TOS, TNG, and DS9 on DVD. But, I recognized it as a addition to SF rather than an end in itself. Oddly, I'm more partial to Star Trek than anything that came after. It did have some unique features -- for media SF anyway. It was more thoughtful, and less dependent on huge explosions and mano et mano encounters between alpha male actors. It tended to accept the strange and novel, rather than cast it in the role of villainy. When it comes to TV SF, I far more enjoyed Red Dwarf to Stargate or the new Babylon 5, which mainly perpetuated science fiction stereotypes.

I am a heretic in regards to media SF. I really do not have a favourite series. Of the super-franchises I, like yourself, prefer Trek over Star Wars. I actually liked Babylon 5 and loved the first 4 series of Red Dwarf. My tastes in media SF are quite eclectic, though I do watch a fair bit of British fare.

The con you mentioned attending in 1974, was probably FanFair III in 1975. There really were no SF cons in Toronto in 1975. There was a comics con up in York University, but only FanFair II and III were held at the King Eddy. FFII was in 1972, I believe.

You are not the only one to comment on this and it would definitely appear to be FanFair III that was my first convention.

I have just about forgotten that nonsense with the fake "Boycott Maplecon" flyer. At the time, I think I may have been editing the OSFiC newszine again, and first we heard of the boycott was Ottawa fandom's outraged reaction. It was astonishing that they took your flyer at face value and never asked anyone what they knew about it. But the OSFS people already had a grudge against the Toronto club, that seems based mainly on misguided attempts to give them advice in the early days. They didn't feel they needed any advice, for one thing. For another, in recommending that a certain individual be take with a grain of salt, that individual took understandable umbrage, and was apparently greatly respected by the OSFS crowd. I guess they had to find out for themselves that he actually was a dork. Whatever... After a couple of years, nobody thought much of the hostility between Toronto and Ottawa fan groups. Some of the people from T.O. went to Maplecon and enjoyed it, some from Ottawa came to Ad Astras and had a good time. Those of us, like myself, who were not greatly into cons, didn't go to either. Frankly, I had better things to do with the money than listen to people yatter about science fiction writers.

Okay, that adds some context to the Maplecon Slandersheet. I was always surprised that OSFS actually believed that OSFiC did write the flyer; the fact that there was an existing feud between the two organisations provides some rational – they wanted to believe that OSFiC was responsible.

I think you exaggerate how pissed off anyone in OSFiC might have been. We were likely more annoyed with OSFS's jumping to conclusions.

I was pretty much out of the loop regarding what went on within Toronto BNFdom at the time. I knew that they were angry about the Slandersheet and about Swill, but all of this came to me third or fourth hand. It was only when I moved to Vancouver that I discovered what a big brouhaha I had created. However, I now believe that this was exaggeration and "broken telephone" of the news travelling the fannish grapevine to Vancouver.

Not really much more to say. Fandom is still around, and some form of it is little to persist -- as you say, people still read books. A slightly younger crowd has taken over running the major conventions, and are eager to follow the same route that Locus and Starship did. They want to be big fish in a bigger pond, with attendance figures a little closer to what SDC and Dragoncon have. To this end, they've been ditching traditional fandom as fast as they can. You won't get any closer to kissing J.K, Rowling's or Tim Power's ass by associating with riff raff, after all. They already dream of the Hugo ceremonies being shown on Fox news. Oh hum. Been there, done that, not too exciting. But some people relish being in the spotlight. After all this time I find I prefer work over schmoozing.

Well, I wouldn't classify traditional fandom as "riff raff". Exactly what do you mean by the term "traditional fandom"? Normally, I would assume that you are referring to literary fandom; however, your comments about SF conventions in general (an activity engaged in by literary fen) may mean you are talking about some segment within literary fandom.

It occurs to me to add that it's no surprise than academics study fandom, and get it wrong. They've been studying it at least since that yobbo, Fredric Wertham, wrote "The World of Fanzines." Presumably, fandom was beneath notice before that. His book was much dreaded when news broke that he had taken an interest in fandom. We assumed it would be a hatchet job, like the one done on comics in the 1950s. In a way, it was worse. Dr. Wertham approved of fanzines and fandom. Unfortunately, he also hadn't a clue about the difference between comics, film and SF fandom, and glibly confused them throughout the book. Like many another expert, he couldn't be bothered to actually ask anyone who might really know the subject to vet his manuscript.

Well, one of the purposes of reviving Swill is to use the fanzine as a form of dialogue between myself and the fanzine segment of SF fandom. In addition to participant observation I will also be conducting a two surveys and a series of formal interviews. Therefore, there will be input from several segments of the current Canadian SF fan community in my study. Wertham's research methods for the World of Fanzines appear to have been based upon an availability sample of fanzines people sent to him – largely from people who didn't know who he was (i.e. they didn't know him as the author of Seduction of the Innocent) – that he performed content analysis on. One of my issues with the entire discipline of psychology is the use of small sample sizes from which the data is then generalised to entire populations or all of humanity without factoring in social and cultural context.

There is, in fact, only one possible distinction that SF fandom has. Not "unity." As you rightly stated, fandom has never been unified, not even when its numbers couldn't possibly have topped a few hundred. But it didn't matter if you had never met Bob Tucker or if you disliked Sam Moskowitz or if you had never read anything by Francis Towner Laney. You knew of them. Likely they knew of you, if you had been around a while and done anything at all of note. Fandom wasn't unified, but it was a fairly tight little community. Other fandoms might be like that, for all I know. All it really takes is to be small enough that everyone is known to everyone else - like a small town. But as special interest groups grow large, this becomes impossible. The fandom goes on, but it becomes more like being a member of Beatles fandom, or table-top railroading, where it is one of maybe hundreds of quite separate communities. For better or worse, SF fandom has long since passed the tipping point.

Yes, that has long since passed. It had already loosing that small town feel in the 1980's and had become regionalised. The success of the genre outside of the print medium has resulted in a substantial growth and change within SF fandom – I think that you will only find that sort of tight community within the segments of SF fandom that remain small, e.g. Canadian fanzine fandom or fans of an obscure (probably foreign) SF series.

Some elements of traditional fandom try to solider on. But they don't control the major institutions of fandom, and are easily marginalized. Most fans have never heard of the names on the Hugo ballots every year, and have no idea who the fan guests of honour are. Many cons have stopped having fan GoHs and have filk guests or costume guests instead. This year's Worldcon in Reno has no Fan GoH. I don't know if that's the first time for a Worldcon or not. It is certainly the way of the future. Personally, I find little satisfaction in being one drop of water in a 40 gallon tub, and prefer the old fandom that was small enough that everyone mattered. It's still around, but graying fast, and no longer very influential with the so-called Big Tent fandom that is evolving.

Again, what do you mean by "traditional fandom"? Certainly literary SF fandom has become "marginalised" in that they are no longer the centre nor do they actively control fandom; they have become a segment of the SF fan subculture.

August 2

Kevin Davies

Hi Neil,

Great to see Swill is back! I've been reading swill@30_9. I agree with what you say about fandom today being "balkanised". It was already happening when we entered fandom.

Hi Kevin. Yes, I agree that the "balkanisation" was already underway when we were the "kids" in the Toronto fan community.

After running GVSTACON in 1979 I was taken aside several times by various 'in the know' fans and given their interpretation of the history of fandom and what was currently going wrong -- rarely what was going right... At that time the big threat was that media fans (of which I was considered one) were infiltrating fandom and 'polluting' *true* literary fandom -- of which the speaker was usually a representative. The other concern was that the new entrants into fandom constituted a 'disturbing force' that was affecting undesirable change to the established order.

Indeed, you evil mediafan. You were a polluter of the "precious bodily fluids" of literary – therefore true – fandom. And I was a fellow traveller; a literary fan that also enjoyed media SF and didn't understand what all of the fuss was about. However, I would take the literary "true fan" stance when confronted with mediafen who believed that series like Battlestar Galactica or Buck Rogers in the 25th Century were the epitome of what SF was and should be. However, I was also uncertain as to what the established order actually was and how one could become a part of it? As I remember, it was more of being part of an age set than anything else; even as a literary fan, one thing was certain, I was too young to ever become a member of the in-group.

This is typical of any closed 'society' or group. There is initially resistance, an attempt at discouraging undesirable activity and conversion ("Get those media fans reading..."), then finally a combination of 'feuds' and resignation (or withdrawal) as the changes inevitably proceed.

Quite correct.

Humans are a tribal species. We are most comfortable when we know the names of everyone in our community and are confident that their opinions and behaviours align with our own. Most also irrationallirrationally assume that their tribe is superior to all others -- it seems to be a human trait designed to comfort ourselves that we've made the 'correct' decision about who to associate with. As soon as any group's membership increases to the point where there are 'strangers in our midst', the social niceties break down and people become increasingly hostile to those they don't know -- also the dilemma of large population centres.

Agreement in part, such as the general concept; disagreement in specifics – but this is not the venue for an academic lecture on the anthropology of social organisation.

As to the question of who is a fan, I believe that one must engage socially with others with shared interests (which may involve one or more fan activities) to be considered a fan (i.e., simply consuming the content that is celebrated by a group of fans is not sufficient to be a part of a 'fandom' for that content).

I have revised my position on this (see Flogging a Dead Trekkie column) which you may still agree with, or perhaps not.

As SF became increasingly popular to the masses through film and TV it attracted ever more people to conventions and clubs, thus accelerating the rate of change and increasing the disaffection experienced by the established 'members' of fandom -- especially as fans divided into smaller special interest groups.

The internet provided the means for all these desperate 'tribes' within fandom to interact without the need to seek the approval of the established fans. Everyone could do their own thing with whoever they wanted to. Special interest associations, 'zines, and conventions thrived. This was bad for the control freaks and those who wanted to see their comfortable status quo preserved (whatever it was); it was great opportunity for everyone else.

Agreed. It allowed for the "gatekeepers" and the control freaks and the fannish thought police to be completely bypassed.

I suspect that mass media and the internet have had this fragmentation effect on many other social groups (e.g., mystery fans, quilters, horror fans, gardeners, costumers, comic fans, car collectors, film fans, gamers, etc.). I see it as a perfectly natural progression of social interaction -- the result of greater access to other like-minded individuals.

Bye for now,

Kevin

August 7, 2011

Lloyd Penney

Dear Neil:

Many thanks for Swill@30 issue 9, and now to see what I can make of it. I have been involved in fandom for nearly 35 years now, and I think that gives me a look into how fandom thinks about itself, and how the older fans are reacting to the newer fans who have discovered this interesting social phenomenon, and are reshaping it in their own interests.

First of all…sorry we didn t connect at Polaris 25. I think we were both pretty busy with what was happening at the convention. I think we will have the chance at SFContario 2.

Yes, we both were. We should be able to meet up at SFContario 2.

I knew about Torcon 2 in 1973…I was living just north of Toronto in Orillia. Of course, I couldn t possibly go, no money, and no understanding parents, anyway. In 1976, I also heard about Toronto Star Trek ' 76, but I couldn t go, same reasons. A move out to Victoria brought VCon to my attention, but still no money. I know some people criticize those who go to various conventions, but the odds of hearing about conventions is greater than hearing about clubs or fanzines.

I don t get this, either. That s why I want Taral to give me a definition for what he calls a "traditional fan". As far as I am concerned, attending conventions is definitely fanac. And for those of us living in the burbs and further out from the cosmopolitan centres back thirty years ago, you would be more likely to hear about a convention than a SF club or fanzine. I only discovered the existence of Bakka through attending conventions in Toronto.

Genre consumers are all of what you list. Years ago, I talked to John Rose, who was then the owner of Bakka Books, the SF bookstore that is still around under a slightly-changed name, and he said that fandom really didn t add much to his book-selling business. He estimated that local fandom gave him less than 10% of his annual business. Casual readers went to Bakka, and they would often leave with several hundred dollars in books. (Couldn t afford that then or now.) John never did think much of fandom, and we didn t really know how little he thought of science fiction until after he sold the store.

I have altered my viewpoint on the genre consumers, slightly… Similar, but also different, situation with the owners of the Occult Shoppe in Toronto; if they had to survive on only the annual business they receive from the Modern Pagan community in Toronto they would have gone bankrupt decades ago.

I am very interested in the psychology of fandom…why we act the way we do, why we treat each others as badly as we do, and why do we tear down each other s efforts. We could be so much better, and build on each other s successes, rather than feel envious and diminished. I have read some of Camille Bacon-Smith s writings, and I came away feeling that my limited time and involvement in Star Trek fandom was in many ways more positive and constructive than my 30+ years in general fandom. Some may complain about the emphasis on literary fandom, but it is the root of fandom as a whole, going back to Gernsback s magazines and the letter column in the late 1920s. Everything must start somewhere. While older fans may complain about fakefans and grousing about the way things used to be, the very first fans had strict' membership requirements… You had to have read every book and magazine out there, and at that time, that was quite possible. You had to correspond with the SF magazines, and finally, you had to have a working science lab in your basement. Not even the old grousing fans qualify for the original fannish credentials.

Hmm... I am more interested in group behaviour than individual behaviour; but then, I m not a psychologist. Literary fandom is indeed the root of SF fandom. Fandom has expanded beyond just literary fandom. I don t except the concept of "fakefans" as it implies that one is pretending to be a fan. If you have been drawn into SF by the series Terra Nova and are now social networking on Facebook about science fiction, and you are totally ignorant about fandom; you are a neo mediafan, end of story. Grousing is of little purpose – it s just an example of the old "in my day, you had to walk five miles to get to school..." rubbish that is always a preamble to making, in one way or another, the statement that something is wrong with the "young people today".

You mention something about how the press will twist whatever is presented to them... no surprise there. I recommend to most conventions to list their conventions in newspaper and magazine listings, but not to invite a member of the press to the convention. The press is not your friend or PR representative. They are there half to get the story, but also entertain the reader; such is the modern press. The press, in covering any science fiction gathering or group will automatically think of us as nerds, geeks, freaks, etc. They rely on old stereotypes that are 40 to 50 years old, and even the young journalists quickly forget their objectivity to make fun of the goofballs in costume. The visual quality of the costume attracts the journalist and photographer, while the more serious and constructive science fiction fan, not nearly as colourful or attractive, will be forgotten, if the journalist and photographer ever knew they were there. Inviting the press to your event means inviting the press to reinforce their old stereotypes, not only for themselves, but to the reader. We are nerds and geeks only because the press has told their readers to think that way. (I have read (and own) the Moskowitz and Warner books you list in your references. Also, I am a graduate of the journalism school at Ryerson University.)

And you also work for the Globe, I think. The average fan is not very colourful; that goes for most of us in society. A buff male in his early twenties in a skimpy Barph the Barbarian costume is colourful for television as potential eye candy and a overweight male in his late thirties wearing a skimpy Barph the Barbarian costume is colourful as "look at the weirdo". The media at a special event are there for a possible interview with a name (e.g. well known author or television star) and for any "colour" – freaks in costume, etc.

I would agree that fandom has been Balkanized into small groups, and that came about by people demanding they the more general fannish groups pay more attention to their interest, and often devote more time and money into promoting it. When the general fannish group is unwilling or unable to comply, other groups break away to form their own clubs and conventions. It s ego and the surety that my interest is superior. When Yvonne and I were busier with local conventions, we tried our best to cross the gaps between the fandoms by assisting with their groups and conventions. When we helped with assembling a labour base for the Toronto in 2003 Worldcon bid, we were able to draw from all the local fandoms, and people who might never have met actually worked together. We tried our best to positive and constructive; often, our efforts were scuttled by vested interests…while we were on the bid for Toronto in 2003, we were not on the committee for Torcon 3. The chairman of the board of directors took a great dislike to Yvonne and after some ridiculous announcements and disciplinary measures that didn't work, I was fired from the committee so he could get rid of both of us. We took the attitude that he really didn't hurt us, but only hurt himself, and we still believe that to be true.

Group politics and status climbing… Whether it's fandom, the SCA, or the Outer Wawa Curling Club, it is always there.

Like anything else society creates to express itself, fandom will change over time. A look at fandom every decade up to the present day shows that the fandom changes, and all the grousing and carping won't change a thing. I regret that some things have changed, but I have met and got to know many of the newer fans that have emerged over the past few years. When I got into local fandom around 1981, many of the established fans sneered at me, and others tried to explain to me why I wasn't a fan and never would be. I am determined not to be the same kind of grumpy old fan for the newcomers.

See what I said to Kevin. The only way I could have been a real fan was to have been born at least ten years earlier…

The letters…I will be digging again for past issues of Swill. I will see what I've got. I think I might have been looking in the wrong box. It is different people staging CanCon 2011, but they know the OSFS crowd, and might be members of OSFS. Good to see there are more issues here. I am trying to be as objective as I can here (my journalism training might help here), but I will try to relay what I feel are the good things about fandom. It's easy to take shots at the pompous and over-important types, but there are also many constructive types who have worked hard to make sure we all enjoy the good times we have.

If you can find some old Swills, that would be wonderful… I agree, there are good things about fandom and a lot of hard work that goes on behind the scenes to organise and run a convention. To be honest, I am still really lounging by the side of the pool with only my toes in the water. Even Polaris was not a complete immersion – as a gafiated literary fan, SFContario will be more of a test…

I just made it to the third page, which is pretty good. Wish we'd gotten together at Polaris, but I think we were both too busy. I think we'll have the time at SFContario. Hope to see you then.

See you at SFContario.

Yours, Lloyd Penney.

Endnote: Quest for Swill

Neil Jamieson-Williams

Okay, here we go. I need to recalibrate my memory, just for my own piece of mind. To that end, I need some old Swills. In particular, the first four issues and especially issue number 1. Alternative texts that may be of aid would be issues 1 through 4 of Miriad and issue 1 (was there more than that) of Nuclear Bunnies.

As always I would appreciate copies of Swill issues 5 and 6 too. And if there are any surviving copies of issues 1 through 3 of Daughter of Swill, Mother or Scum I will gladly receive them.

While it is probably easiest, these days, to scan these old zine and send them via email -- I would be happy to reimburse any photocopying and postage costs if that is preferred.

Thanks in advance.

Research Project Note:

Due to the changes and new guidelines, I was unable to submit my application this Fall. I will have to wait until next Fall and hope that the Conservatives do not do to the SSHRC (Social Sciences and Humanities Research Council) what they have don't to the National Research Council; they gutted their funding. Perhaps SSHRC will do better as they do not do natural science research of the sort that doesn't support the Conservative Party ideologies that the Earth is a mere 10,000 years old and that burning fossil fuels is good for the environment. We will see where the axe will fall.

In the meantime, I will continue to conduct pre-research research out of pocket.

Planned "Pith Helmet and Propeller Beanie" tour 2011/2012:

- SFContario   November 2011

- Ad Astra   April 2012

- Polaris   July 2012

- Sci Fi Fan Expo   August 2012

Original image determined to be too dark and would create bleed-through ((

Original image was a defacement of the poster for V-Con 36.

SWILL

@ 30

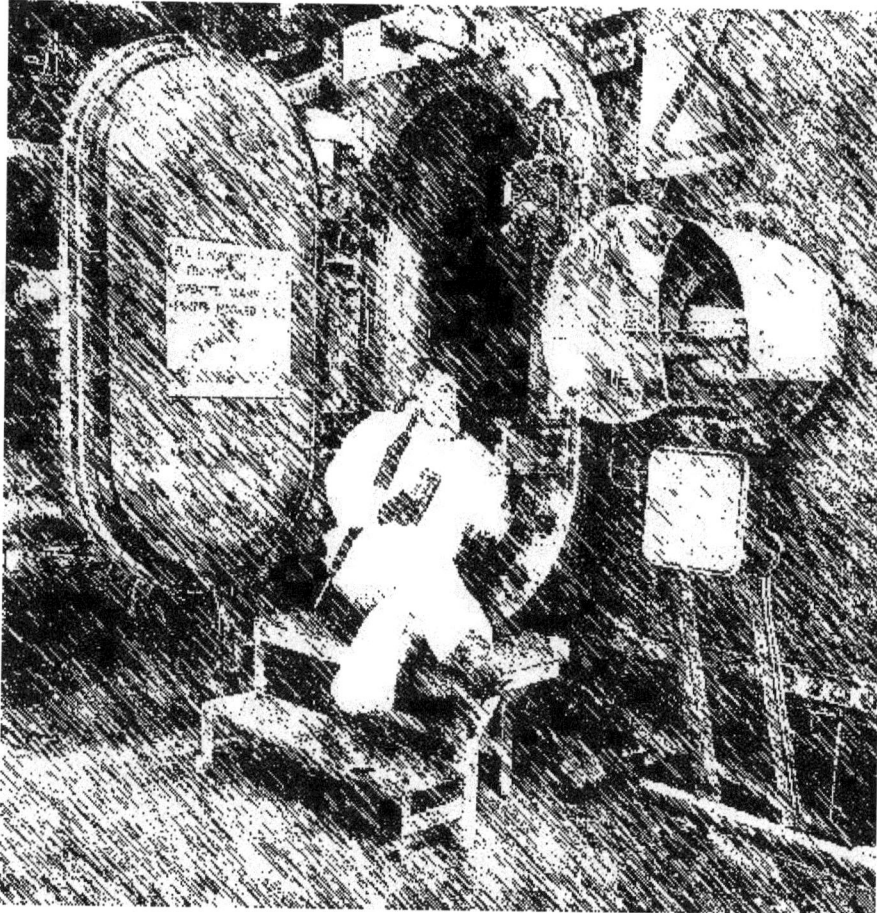

#11   Winter 2011

Table of Contents

Swill @ 30 is published quarterly (Spring, Summer, Autumn, and Winter) along with an annual every February – in other words, five times per year.

Swill @ 30

Issue #11 Winter 2012

Copyright © 1981 - 2012 VileFen Press

a division of Klatha Entertainment an Uldune Media company

swill.uldunemedia.ca

Editorial: Past Imperfect

Neil Jamieson-Williams

It's a funny thing, memory -- it is neither as clear nor as correct as we often think it is. And then, sometimes it is. While there are still some anomalies[1] regarding my recall of Maplecon, the droogs at Maplecon, and the first issue of Swill, more evidence has emerged since the last issue. Thanks to Lester Rainsford[2] whom I ran into at SFContario 2. Lester still had the "Swill archive" that I left with him when I went out to BC back in May of 1981. This was not a complete Swill archive, I did have a Swill archive that included copies of all issues of the original Swill, the mimeo stencils of issues #3 through #6, copies of Daughter of Swill, Mother of Scum, and an assorted selection of issues of BeSwill. Unfortunately, due to a basement flood (actually more of a localised, persistent basement leak) the archive, along with my wife's collection of cooking magazines, all had to be tossed out as they had been reduced to one single black mould mass. The "Swill archive" in Lester's possession included copies of issues #1[3] and #2 of Swill, the mimeo stencils for those two issues, and other assorted stuff.[4]

Nevertheless, it now beyond doubt that the Maplecon Slandersheet was printed and distributed at Maplecon III in 1980. This fits my earlier recollection of events; more or less, for the most part, more. However, timelines are not my greatest interest this time around. My focus is on content. It has been close to seventeen years since I last looked at issues #1 and #2 of Swill. And in this case, my memory has been imperfect: I remembered Swill as being far worse than it actually was.

First of all, the typeface was not as bad as I recalled it to be. Lester's electric typewriter was clean in its typeface with no visibly dirty keys. In contrast, my old manual typewriter had several dirty keys but was nowhere near as bad as the pudmonkey font. (And just to cut off any discussion/whining -- Graeme, Lloyd, and Taral -- regardless of this revelation; the pudmonkey font stays.) The mimeographed copies from the archive are a little smudgy; which is why they were preserved -- the cleaner copies were distributed.

As for the content, I may have to eat my own words. In issue #8 I said, "At its core, the spirit of Swill was a shock and awe boot to the head at science fiction fandom. Vicious, angry, intentionally offensive, silly, irreverent, and obnoxious; brimming with the malicious delight of a shock-jock gadfly screaming with feigned anger – all sound and fury... but was it anything more

---

[1] Such as, did I attend more than one Maplecon?
[2] Lester has returned as of this issue as the columnist for Pissing on a Pile of Old Amazings.
[3] These copies would be of the second print run of issue #1 the first run was by photocopy.
[4] Such as, the second issue of Reticulum and the two issues of Sirius.

than prose version of smashing windows and tossing a few Molotov cocktails?" Uhm...not really. Even by 1981 standards the original Swill is tame. There is no shock and awe, no Molotov cocktails, nor even any broken windows -- it's more of flaming shit bag. Issues #1 & #2 definitely were intentionally offensive, silly, and obnoxious but no actual boot to the head to fandom. That said, the ultra-serious members of fandom, those who viewed fandom as an ideal community and FIAWOL as a sacred act, may have perceived Swill in 1981 somewhat the way I described it in issue #8.

I also say in issue #8, "The spirit of Swill was critical and blunt and intentionally malicious and its target was SF and SF fandom. The odd thing is that some – not much, but some – of that criticism was and remains valid...however, those nuggets that were and are still valid are not unique insights of Swill. They are not necessarily well thought out arguments – kind of like a vulgar and poorly written Rick Mercer rant." Well some of that is true and some of that is not. Most of the content in issues #1 & #2 do read like a vulgar Mercer rant and the arguments contained are not usually well constructed; however, when we offering a critique, we were actually saying something. And some of our comments were indeed, unique for the time period. Other times, we were really just being humorous, though some fans would not appreciate the joke, e.g. The Average S.F. Fan (aka the fat fan article) and the "Guest Editorial" -- both in issue #2.

I had been told that the Maplecon Slandersheet is blatantly homophobic by those who recall it. I'm not certain about that claim. There are two lines in the Slandersheet that can be viewed as homophobic; though I would question the interpretation that these two lines are "blatantly homophobic" by 2012 standards, let alone those of 1981. It was very much the intention of the Slandersheet to be offensive, with a particular focus of comic book fans, comic book collectors, and used book/comic book dealers -- though it can also be viewed as being offensive to capitalists, sloths, swine, toads, and gays. I am willing to admit that the Slandersheet does contain two lines that can be interpreted as being mildly homophobic by today's standards for which I offer a mild apology; though I refuse to hang my head in shame or do any further penance for what I co-wrote 31 years ago.

It is good to read the original Swill once more – based on issues #1 & #2; I have to say I am proud to have been the editor and a writer for this fanzine.

Thrashing Trufen Themes Past and Present

Neil Jamieson-Williams

Having now had a chance to reread, several times, issues #1 & #2 of Swill – as well as re-reading Swill Online (#7) – it is clear that there are some reoccurring and persistent themes that Swill has focused on, both in the past and at present. The title this new column casts light on one of those themes; the issue of the trufan – and yes, in the opinion of Swill they deserve to be thrashed (actually thrashing may be too good for them).

The entire concept of the trufan is absolute shit to begin with. The term, by the act of existing, implies that some fans are "better" than others and that there are fans who are not "real fans" – aka, the fakefan. And who are those who determine who are the trufen and who are the fakefen? Usually some, self-appointed, self-designated, elite group -- who are all bona fide, in their own opinion, trufen -- that then designates, as an authority, who are the non-trufen "real fans" and which untouchable sudras are the "fakefans". This form of categorisation is always highly subjective and often accompanied by loud axe-grinding in the background. While this type of behaviour is not unique to SF fandom (I have seen similar behaviour occur among Modern Pagans, punk rockers, and software developers), it has the least amount of validity when applied to SF fans. My position, which is the Swill position, is that any person who regularly enjoys reading/viewing SF genre content and whom identifies themself as being a SF fan, is a SF fan. This ideal-type fan could be entirely devoted to original series Star Trek (never watching any of the later series) or they could be a fanzine writer or they could have interests in a wide variety of written and media SF content as well as the fan subculture itself, e.g. fanzines, con-running. There are different segments of the SF fan subculture and different levels of involvement and different criteria as to what are the most important aspects of being a SF fan -- which in turn produce different definitions of what is a SF fan, which result in the movers-and-shakers within each of the myriad segments self-defining themselves a "trufans". Therefore, a trufan is a social construct created by an elite group that defines that particular elite and is used to engage in impression management that generates ephemeral status that is accorded to that elite group and its membership;[5] trufen have been the perfect target for Swill assualt in the past and will continue to be in the future.

Another major theme is this: if there really is such a creature as a trufan (of SF) that species exists outside of the SF fandom population. What I mean is that those persons who regularly and actively support the genre financially, through purchase of genre content that are not part of the SF fandom population -- who don't identify themselves as SF fans -- are, if the term can be applied to anybody, the real trufen. That the genre consumers, who would appear to most fans as nothing more than "mundanes", are the majority and a majority that either has a low opinion of SF fandom or is indifferent to SF fandom's existence. I have called these people "readers" in the past but have switched to the more inclusive term of genre consumers. These people are neither "mundanes" nor "fakefans" in the context to the genre itself; on the contrary, they are very important to the genre and perhaps more important that the SF fan population itself. Within the context of the SF fandom subculture, though; they range between being nonentities to "antifans"[6]. Regardless, genre consumers are important and Swill will continue to offer support for the genre consumer.

One of the old themes of the original Swill was a negative bias toward comic book and media SF fans. In the case of media SF fans the argument was that these fans had little knowledge of the written genre which preceded the growth of media SF and believed that all the major SF tropes had emerged with media SF -- in particular, with Star Trek. The secondary argument was that most of the media SF in the early 1980's was best described as space opera[7] and often very bad space opera.[8] While there was some good media SF, most of it was not. From the standpoint of 2012, most of the media SF today is superior overall that that of 1982, but there remain stinkers, e.g. Terra Nova (2011). Any attack on media SF today will be tempered by two governors; one, the increased quality of most media SF, and second, the editor/writer has had experience writing/producing media SF. Nevertheless, media SF will receive praise when it is deserved and a thorough tolchocking when it offers the viewer complete shite. The negative bias of the original Swill remains for the majority of comic books that again borrow tropes from literary SF

[5] Translation: trufan is a term created in the course of social interaction by a group of individuals who see themselves as an elite and use the trufan term to identify their group. This is then used to create the impression among outsiders that that the group and its membership hold the status of being trufen; the status is ephemeral as it only has potential value within the SF fandom subculture and is meaningless and/or a mark of reduced status within the larger culture, e.g. Sci-Fi geek.

[6] More on this in Flogging a Dead Trekkie...

[7] I confess, I do like space opera. I like old space opera like that of A. Bertram Chandler, James H. Schmitz, and others. I also like the "new" space opera of Verner Vinge, F. Peter Hamilton, Alistair Reynolds, and others.

[8] For example, in print Perry Rhodan, in media the original Battlestar Galactica, and Buck Rogers in the 25th Century...

5

and claim them as original and for the deplorable low quality of what passes as science within comic book science fiction. Bias regarding graphic novels is also negative, but approaching neutral, with each graphic novel being judged on a case to case basis. And overall, magna and anime both suffer from the same ills as Western comic books; though when doing fantasy they can do a good job, but most of their SF is really science fantasy.

The final theme that I will discuss is that of critiquing the genre -- usually the publishers (and also the production companies) of SF content. This will not change in the current Swill and will be more hard ass and systematic than in the original Swill. There are already several targets in sight that will be fired upon in future issues.

So, although the present incarnation of Swill will be used as an outlet for organising my research project of SF fandom and as a forum through which to dialogue with that segment of fandom known as fanzine fandom; it is going to get a lot less academic in the future issues. Swill is getting its edge back.

Pissing on a Pile of Old Amazings:

...a modest column by Lester Rainsford

I am informed that deadlines loom and a column is due. So here is the column.

Deadlines?? I understand that Valdimir Illych succeeded due to organization and no doubt deadlines, but they seem kinda antithetical to anarchy. Where "I understand" means "I think I heard somewhere, and can't be arsed to look it up on wikipedia".

The problem with pissing on a pile of old Amazings, or old Swills, besides needing more beer (that's a problem?) is that you can't tell the difference between high acid paper anyway. Which is to say, what was radical and daring may only seem so at the time, and not so much afterwards. Plus, one person's shit disturber is another person's asshole, and when it's a value judgment of the judgment impaired, well.

So we can look back to First Swill (times). Harloan Ellison, Shit Disturber or Asshole? Well I think people have figured this out by now. I am sad to hear that Joanna Russ died. I am sure some people thought she was an asshole but they're probably assholes so who cares. The current provocateurs du jour seem to be Baen barflies, and there seems no doubt even today where they come down on the divide there. So who are the real shit distubers today? Damned if I know, at the recent con we discussed new wave and cyberpunk which everyone agrees are dead as doornails and long gone. But today cucsk so that (and not in a good way) we go back and rehash stuff that happened in our youth if we are old. and if we are youg, then apparently we dress up in this 'steampunk' thing. Oddly, steampunk devotees apparently haven't really looked at the past because boy things were dirty in teh age of coal, but their costumes are all immaculate white shirt and pressed vests. I guess seteampunkers aren't planning to be members of the 'black gang'. This was the bunch who actually kept your triple expansion reciprocating engine dreatdought steaming at a crazyass 17 knots. There's a reason that the real Dreadnought went to turbine and Chruchill pushed through oil-fired boilers for the Grand Fleet and it wasn't because Britain had lots of oil and no coal.

I really hope that in twenty or thirty years people at cons won't be discussing the rise and fall of steampunk although from a brief trip throguh the bookstore prior to Christmas it seems that a number of authors are making a good liviing putting out steam-fired swill. I shudder to think of what a boiler leak would be like in a coal fired swill-ship but I expect those steampunk goggles to actually come in handy although a good rubber gas mask may be a more appropriate costume accessory. As for using Swill to power your swillship, i have some news for you, it WAS low-acid paper. So beware.

Flogging a Dead Trekkie:

Odds and Sods...

Neil Jamieson-Williams

This time around I will just tidy a few things up and all that...

First up, All About Swill revised:

Swill #1
(February, 1981) Cover Art: Neil Jamieson-Williams this was a badly drawn self-caricature of Neil holding a bottle of beer in his left hand and a cigarette, while giving "the finger" with his right (the "stubby" beer bottle is not well drawn and the perspective is off so it actually looks like a pill bottle). Title composed of punk-style newspaper headline cut-out letters. Editorial by Neil; article by Neil called MediaFen Suck; Pissing on a Pile of Old Amazings by Lester Rainsford; Fun and Games (Thrash the Trekkie) written by Rainsford using the name Scrotum the Unbathed and reviewed by Neil and Steve Vano; a reprint of the Maplecon Slandersheet; some fake LoCs; and the back cover – same as the front cover.

Swill #2
(March, 1981) Cover Art: Neil Jamieson-Williams and Lester Rainsford – depicts three piles of shit, the one in the foreground labelled "Fandom" with lots of flies circling around it (preferred by more flies than other forms of shit). Editorial by Jamieson-Williams and Rainsford using the name Reverand B. Jeramiha Jones on smut in SF and SF fandom; an article by Jamieson-Williams on Fen Art; Pissing on a Pile of Old Amazings attacks cigarette smoking and the discipline of Chemistry; article inspired by Hoyt and written by Rainsford and Jamieson-Williams and attributed to J. S. Goobly titled The Average SF Fan (the infamous fat fan article); article by Jamieson-Williams titled They Space Tribbles, Don't They advocating the death of OSFiC; the very first Stephano (Steve Vano) My Fame strip; Lester Rainsford's The American Weigh: Or, A Gram of Brains is Worth a Pound of Shit which attacks Libertarian Party SF, Libertarian Party SF Fandom, and some of the determinist claims made by the political philosophy of

the Libertarian Party; actual real LoCs – only one is semi-fake which is a Swill writer to writer response; back cover that proclaims that Physics Rules OK.

Second up, SFContario 2 Con Report:

This was a smallish convention, with a focus on literary science fiction. The convention programming was above average and there was enough to do most of the time. The dealers room was not the best as it was in two parts and "off the beaten track"; there was nothing but dealers on this part of the convention floor. It would have been better if one of the dealers rooms had been used for panels to draw people over to this section of the convention floor -- I understand that this was how it was done for SFContario 1 and had been changed for accessibility issues. The AE - The Canadian Science Fiction Review anniversary party on Friday was great but the Saturday night dance was a bust as there was no liquor licence for the event (there had been for the AE party) and almost everybody ended up going downstairs to the hotel bar. Overall, a nice little con that I do recommend for the literary fans -- I will be attending SFContario 3.

And finally, AntiFan:

In my naive youth I had always thought that this was an established trope in SF fandom in an old Spy vs Spy manner. The figure of AntiFan was dressed in black with a cloak and 17th century hat -- like Spy vs Spy or Guy Fawkes -- and had a wide variety of various explosive devices. I remember these cartoons from fanzines in the early 1980's and, as the editor of Swill, I embraced the AntiFan concept. It was a surprise that I recently discovered that the character of AntiFan was not something that went back to the 1960's or earlier but a creation of the Australia in 83 WorldCon bid. Supporters of the ConStellation bid (Baltimore) were agents of AntiFan while those who supported the AusiCon bid were trufen -- the trufen lost this one. Nevertheless, I hope to dig up some of those AntiFan cartoons and repurpose them for Swill, or something along that line…

Scribbling on the Bog Wall:
Letters of Comment

Neil Jamieson-Williams

As I write this, there is only two LoCs this time around. As always, my comments are in red.

From: "Taral Wayne" <Taral@teksavvy.com>

Subject: Re: Swill @ 30 Issue #10 Autumn 2011

Date: Tue, November 1, 2011 2:55 pm

To: swill@uldunemedia.ca

_____

I'll have to see if I can define "traditional fan" for you later. It has nothing to

do with whether or not a fan goes to conventions, by the way. I didn't involve the

issue of cons because they weren't relevant in that sense. Fans have been going to

cons since 1936... I've gone to a few, myself.

_____

Hi Taral,

I think that you provided me with the definition at SFContario 2 – your definition of traditional fan appears to be very similar to the concept of a core fan; a person who is a genre consumer, self identifies themselves as a fan, participates in fan activity, and is integrated into a local geographic fan community that operates as a primary social network. Am I correct?

And yes, in our society, any group like this is under threat – not because of the rise of media SF fandom, but due to techno-culture changes within the society as a whole.

1706 -24 Eva Rd.
Etobicoke, ON
M9C 2B2

November 22, 2011

Dear Neil:

It's taken me a couple of days to get myself together after the SFContario 2
weekend, but if nothing else, everything else is sorted out, or put away, or
in the laundry, etc., so I can finally catch up with a sudden mountain of
fanzines to deal with and comment on. With that in mind, here are comments
on Swill @ 30, issue 10.

(I should ask what was the response at the convention to your
questionnaire, and what they thought of the fanzine. A lot of the people
there know that I am connected with fanzines, but few of them are interested
in them themselves. Glad you got yourself the first two Swills, even if they
are photocopies.)

Hi Lloyd,

Well the mix-up with printing meant that I had no surveys with me at the convention. As it is,
the survey will be redesigned anyway and will go live sometime in March.

The copies of Swill #1 and #2 that I got from Lester Rainsford were not photocopies but actual
mimeographed copies, albeit a little smudgy.

I am certain I saw the droogs at some local convention in Toronto…whether it
was Adam and Kevin and you, or others, I am not sure. It must have been you,
now that I think of it, because I do remember poor Fritz being abused. I
have to wonder who the overweight Trekkies were, and it may be likely that
given my own interests of that distant time, I might have known them.

Why is everybody so concerned with "poor Fritz"? Fritz was a pile of clothing (usually stuffed
with hotel linens) and a Styrofoam wig head; a collection inanimate objects. But yes, we did
abuse Fritz horrorshow. I have no idea as to the identity of the overweight Trekkies, only that
they were there.

Conventions do have a structure of some kind, and that structure may depend

12

on the subject matter of the convention. One friend who goes to mostly media SF conventions found that the literary SFContario she attended was quite odd, and very different. For myself, I found it a bit of a throwback to the way literary conventions were run in the 80s and 90s, and it was strangely familiar, and quite enjoyable. Polaris is a different convention from what it was in the 80s and 90s, too. As we age, our expectations of such a convention change, so if you didn't like it before, give it five years or so, and the changes may be to your liking. These days, because I've worked in the evening for some years, I haven't watched any evening SF television, not much has attracted me at all, and I have seen few SF movies, so the demand to meet actors doesn't really turn me on. Polaris has turned into a steampunk costuming occasion, and for the last few years, an opportunity to be a dealer and sell some goods to the membership. (Any parties at the convention were staged by the convention itself; there seems to be a vague hostility towards any parties staged by attendees, promoting their own group, project, event or convention.)

I liked SFContario, but then I am a literary fan first and a media fan second. I can see how it would seem strange to a media fan though. It is kind of like an old fashioned relaxicon with more programming. As I never attended any of the Toronto Treks I cannot compare between Polaris now and then; though I would hazard a speculation that it was more Trek-based in the past and now caters to a variety of SF & F media. Steampunk costuming is a current fad, in five years it will be replaced by something else. Yes, I noticed that there was strict room party control at Polaris – though, I had been told that this was being done to keep the hotel happy…

I found out a while ago where the term 'cosplay' comes from. It's a relatively new term to me, but was invented by a Japanese journalist who covered the 1984 Worldcon in Anaheim, California. He saw people in costume perhaps acting out a generic scene from the TV show or movie the costumes came from, and he nicknamed is cosplay, or costuming play, from perhaps the acting style of play or perhaps play as in having fun, not really sure.

It is interesting isn't it? Back in the old days a good group costume usually involved some form of acting out in character. This has really taken off in the anime community.

I have been both a lit fan and a mediafan…these days, mostly lit. Because my own involvement in fandom goes back to the late 70s, I would have to describe myself as a traditional fan and an active fan.

We will discuss this next issue as I will be revising the categories…

Gotta agree with Uncle Swill...fanzines may be an old way of communicating, but it's the participation that people like about it. Some do say that the letters of comment are optional, but the decision to not have a letter column gets them in trouble with others. Myself, I think a letter column is preferable, but I am biased. I have received zines with no letter column, and I have responded to them anyway. It's the communication that's important, not the byline.

Yes, I like having a letter column too. And, as the original Swill had one, I have to keep with tradition. By the way, I have commented to Askance on your review of Swill @ 30...

My loc...yes, we did connect up at SFContario 2...I hope I actually had something of substance to say. Yvonne and I had been in the Vaughan St. store a long time ago, but recently, we did have a look in the new store on Bathurst St., and it is, unfortunately, a shadow of what it once was. Believe me, I don't like the idea of calling others fakefans, for that's more tearing down the efforts of others.

And for building up the ephemeral status of fannish elites...

Indeed, I work at the Globe in the evenings, not as a reporter, but as a data entry clerk. We do intend to attend Ad Astra 2012 and Polaris 26 in the new year, and perhaps we can talk more, and see what else there is to discuss through questionnaires, or just a general discussion.

Take care, and see you with the next issue. Might not be until 2012, so the best of Christmases and New Years...might be a little early.

Hope that you both had a happy holiday season and all the best for 2012. See you at Ad Astra...

Yours, Lloyd Penney.

Endnote: Narrowing the Lens

Neil Jamieson-Williams

Research Notes:

At this point in the research project I appear to have come to the same realisation that previous researchers also must have reached; fandom is way to big to easily study. That said, I will not follow the solution taken by others who have gone before -- to limit my study to one group within fandom, and only one group. However, I am going to narrow my focus and place primary emphasis on two particular groups within the SF fan subculture; conrunners and fanzine fandom. At the same time I will continue to research the whole SF fan culture. It also means that there will be two research projects operating simultaneously. The larger one will focus on conrunners (and event organisers) and the segments of the SF fan subculture that their conventions/events are aimed at and the smaller study will be on fanzine fandom. The rationale behind this is that by organising my research project this way I am more likely to receive funding from SSHRC (Social Sciences and Humanities Research Council).

Part of the change in regulations that have been made to SSHRC is a new emphasis on applied research, or that there is an applied component to the research. I have decided, based on my earlier special events research, that by placing emphasis on SF fan conrunners I can also collect data on convention/event organiser relations with the venue operators, attendee relations with the venue operators, that would provide an applied component to the study; i.e. data that would be useful to the hospitality industry. It is also a useful structure for the research in that, one speculates (though one could be in error) that the conrunners for successful conventions probably know a fair bit about the type of fan who is drawn to their particular convention -- in other words, that they know their audience. This would make them strong candidates for key imformants in the research project. Therefore, the major research project would be structured thus:

- Interviews with conrunners, either face-to-face or electronically

- Participant observation (if permitted) at concom meetings prior to and after each convention studied

- Participant observation at each convention

- Online survey of conrunners

- Online surveys of fans

- Interviews -- electronically -- with fans

Plus; interviews with venue operators and online surveys of venue operators

The **Pith Helmet and Propeller Beanie Tour** tentatively will be:

2011 -- 2014

Polaris 25, SFContario 2, Ad Astra 31, Polaris 26, Sci Fi Fan Expo 2012, SFContario 3, FilKONtario 23, Anime North 2013, Polaris 27, V-Con 38, SFContario 4, FutureCon 4, Ad Astra 33, WesterCon 2014, Worldcon 2014, SFContario 5.

The fanzine fandom study will be done out of pocket and is a sidebar to the major research project.

The **Continuing Quest for Swill...**

While it is wonderful that issues #1 and #2 have been recovered, there are more issues remaining to be found and scanned. Issues #3 through #6 are most wanted. Any surviving copies of Daughter of Swill, Mother of Scum Issues #1 through #3 would also be appreciated.

Original image determined to be too dark and would create bleed-through ((

Original image was a defacement of the poster for the 2011 Futurecon New Year's Eve Party

SWILL

@ 30

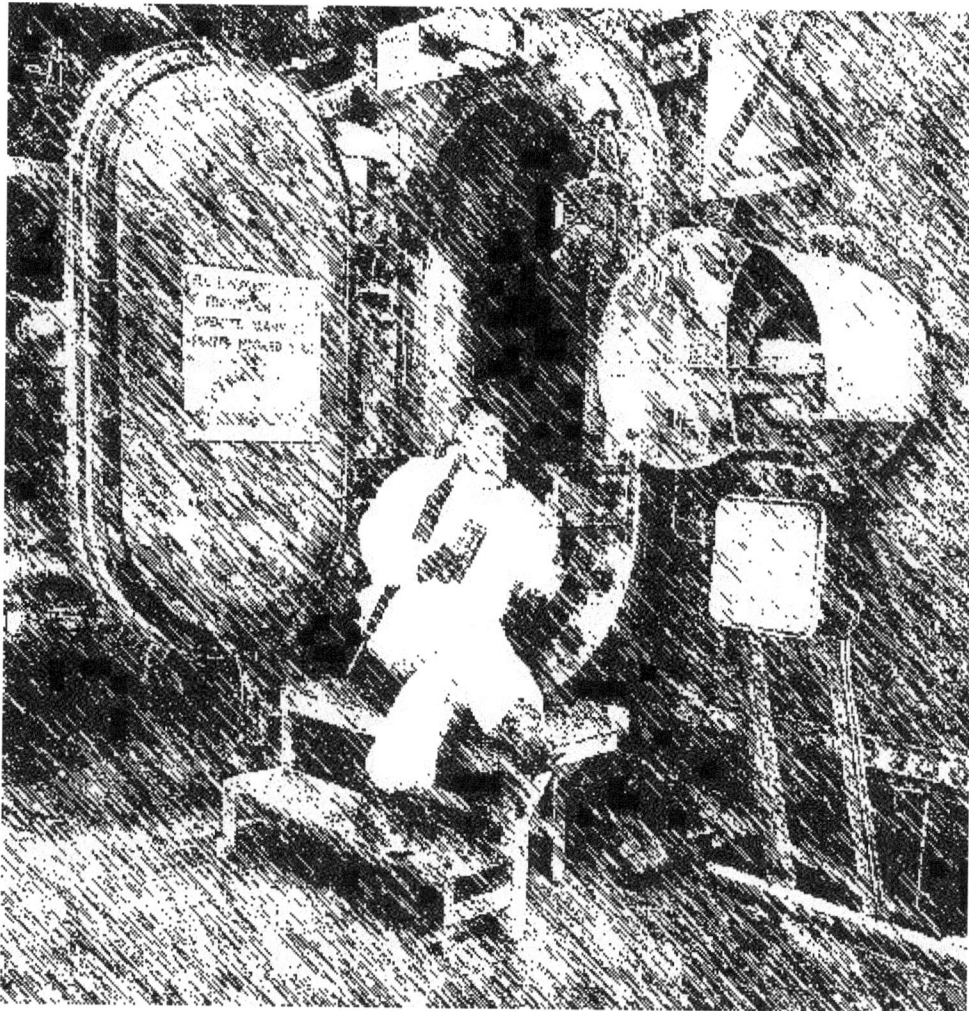

#12   Annual — February 2012

Table of Contents

Swill @ 30 is published quarterly (Spring, Summer, Autumn, and Winter) along with an annual every February – in other words, five times per year.

Swill @ 30 Annual

Issue #12 February 2012

Copyright © 1981 - 2012 VileFen Press

a division of Klatha Entertainment an Uldune Media company

swill.uldunemedia.ca

Editorial: Goose-Stepping Toward Tomorrow

Neil Jamieson-Williams

What I am about to discuss is not new – it has been said before and has probably been stated better than I am about to do so here. Nevertheless, onward… There is an unfortunate and strong authoritarian undercurrent within science fiction.

This was well illustrated in Norman Spinrad's 1972 novel, The Iron Dream. In an alternate timeline Adolph Hitler immigrated to America after the Great War (there is no WWII in this timeline), and used his modest artistic skills to become first a pulp-science fiction illustrator and later a successful science fiction writer and editor. Hitler would die from a cerebral haemorrhage caused by tertiary syphilis in 1953, shortly after writing his most popular novel, Lord of the Swastika. The majority of The Iron Dream is Hitler's Lord of the Swastika, post-apocalypse action tale in a lurid 1940's pulp style. Spinrad's conceit is that the reader is drawn into the storyline and ends up rooting for the protagonist, all the while, in the background is the nagging knowledge from the reader's mind reminding them that what they are cheering on is Nazism.

Ursula K. LeGuin in her 1975 essay "American SF and the Other" also touches on this theme as she questions the preference for, "authoritarianism, the domination of ignorant masses by a powerful elite…democracy is quite forgotten. Military virtues are taken as ethical ones… It is a perfect baboon patriarchy…" Far from science fiction being a literature of ideas LeGuin states that the preference for authoritarian social organisation is, "brainless regressivism." And I agree, the passion for authoritarianism in SF is a retreat to pre-human primate social organisation.

In my 1984 fanzine, Daughter of Swill, Mother of Scum[1] I devoted the first issue to this subject of authoritarianism and the fascination that science fiction has for the fascist ethic. As I have no copies of this issue[2], I can only go by recollection; I rehash LeGuin and Spinrad though I don't think that I offered any new ideas to the discussion.

So, if these issues have been raised in the past why am I harping about them now? Because, those issues not only remain, they have become worse over time.

---

[1] There were three issues of this fanzine, each issue was an essay-like rant on a particular topic.
[2] Or any of the three issues. Again, a request to fans in British Columbia who may have copies of this zine in their collections; please scan a copy and email it to me.

Science fiction continues to have a love for authoritarianism, whether it is based upon heredity (monarchy/genetic castes), gender (patriarchy/matriarchy), the State (communism/fascism), the military (dictatorship), or capital (corporate oligarchy).[3] It is not uncommon for there to be a blend between different authoritarian foundations, but in the end, the result is still authoritarian. An additional theme and favourite is paternalism – this appears to be very common in American science fiction. The supreme leader is simultaneously a cuddly grandfather figure and absolute dictator. Authoritarianism is seen as normative and futuristic. And whatever evil authoritarian regime it is that the bad guys rule, upon close examination, the good guys (all those captains, majors, commanders, resistance leaders, etc.) are just as authoritarian and anti-democratic – the good guys just don't eat kittens and babies for breakfast. True, the good guy protagonist is usually a maverick, someone who doesn't always follow the rules, who isn't "by the book"; this supposedly makes them individualistic and democratic. Really? It does single them out as being individualistic, but it doesn't necessarily make them democratic; even though they are violating the prime directives of their superiors, the protagonist still expects their subordinates to follow the orders that they give them without question. This does not bring to mind a person who is democratic; it brings to mind a person who is so individualistic that they believe that the rules do not apply to them, that they are above the law – this is the viewpoint common with many an absolute monarch.

Among all these heroes and leaders and so on... Where are the people? LeGuin asks the same question back in 1975, "Are they ever *persons*, in SF? No... The people, in SF, are not people. They are masses, existing for one purpose: to be led by their superiors." It is always about the leaders and the leaders have little taste for actual democracy. Where are the elected parliaments and assemblies?

When democracy does appear in science fiction, it tends to take one of two forms, neither of which are really positive. One form of democratic organisation that is common in SF is the "council", a form that is only in part democratic. These councils tend to be populated by high status individuals who act as representatives (we usually are not told how one becomes a member of the council, perhaps they are voted in or perhaps not). Yes, these organisations do run quasi-democratically, they have votes on issues, much the same as any corporate board of directors does, but are they actually representative. How representative is a council of 15, even if the members are elected by the populace, for a planetary population of 4 billion? I would say, not very. When actual assemblies do appear they are farcical parodies of the UN General Assembly; this is to demonstrate that the democratic institutions have been corrupted by politicians and outside groups, which is why we need the strong leadership of the protagonist to clean things up (Adolph Hitler had a similar view on elected parliaments and assemblies). Although science fiction, in particular American science fiction, pays lip service (akin to ritual religious observance) to democracy, there is s strong distrust for democracy in science fiction.

---

[3] A corporation is not a democratic organisation; it has a one-way flow of decision-making, from the top down.

The thing is, humans actually have a strong preference for democracy. For the vast majority of our tenure on this planet we have lived within democratic social structures; this only began to change with the development of food production, aka agriculture. Agriculture first emerged around 10,000 years ago and for the first several thousand years it was small scale – often referred to as garden-plot agriculture or horticulture – and was not destructive to democratic social structures. It did damage human democracy, though. Food production resulted in sedentary living (the first villages/towns), that resulted in food surpluses, that would produce inequality, that would lead to forms of local governance other than direct democracy. In some cultures, authoritarian rule would emerge at this time; but in most, some form of democracy or quasi-democracy would remain.

Around 7,000 the first shifts began that, for some cultures, moved them from horticulture to intensive agriculture – with an emphasis on cereal grains. Those cultures that made the switch to intensive agriculture also made the switch from some form of democratic social organisation to authoritarianism. That is because under intensive agriculture, some powerful group always sets themselves up as being the nobility who own all the land by divine right; everybody else, that is the bulk of the population, are commoners and the commoners who are at the lowest rank in the social hierarchy, again this is the majority of the population, are now serfs or slaves who work the land for the nobles. The development and spread of intensive agriculture coincides with what is often termed, the rise of civilisation; indeed, it was within these cultures that innovations such as forging bronze, writing, and the classical developments in engineering and architecture appear.

While the norm for these civilisations was authoritarianism[4], some democratic practice was tolerated. Not much, but some. Usually this would be permitted at the local level where the free men, not the serfs or villains[5], could elect their own town leaders. There were two reasons why authoritarian leaders would allow this. The first being that from the perception of the elite, whatever the free commoners did in their towns was of little or no importance. Second, it was more efficient; it saved the elite from having to expend resources as well as the bother of governing these towns. As we entered the Modern period[6], authoritarian leaders do attempt to roll the clock back on these freedoms, due to excesses of liberty busting out all over Europe. Excesses such as all that free thought breaking out all over the place due to all these books to read due to the moveable type printing press… Especially when this free thinking results in dissent and chaos in the form of the Protestant Reformation, the Counter-Reformation, the Wars

---

[4] Okay, the Roman Republic is an exception, in part. During the Republic there were elected assemblies and the senate, but the representation was somewhat gerrymandered so that patricians (the Roman elite) always would have a controlling block. The Republic was quasi-democratic, in my opinion.
[5] Inhabitant of a village; a small community on a noble's lands where the commoners bound to that particular noble would live. Towns on the other hand existed on lands outside of any noble's estate.
[6] Historians disagree as to when the Modern period begins, but the majority agree that by 1500 CE it has begun.

4

of Reformation, and the English Civil War. In the aftermath there is the Industrial Evolution[7], which accelerates the pace of production, and creates the oxymoron of the wealthy commoner – all of which sets the stage for the American and French Revolutions; democracy bursting out all over. The 20th century brought forth new industrial forms of authoritarianism in the form of fascism and communism, though even these totalitarian authoritarian forms of government, had some difficulty removing all democratic elements from society; for example, there were still municipal elections during the Third Reich[8]. Humans like democracy; we choose it readily when it is not a danger to do so and still tend to choose it when it is dangerous to make that choice.

Of course, since the end of the Cold War, authoritarianism has been on the rise within the Western democracies. Civil liberties have been eroded (for our own safety), social programmes gutted, the average wage continues to shrink, the middle class is in decline, while our politicians vote themselves substantial pay increases, and our corporate CEOs hire analysts to recommend that annual compensation is inadequate and must be increased, the right to strike and collective bargaining is being curtailed, and the financial sector was permitted (due to the relaxing of government regulation) to create the worst recession since the Great Depression and handed the taxpayer, i.e. the average citizen the bill. The current trends point toward a more authoritarian future, everywhere. Perhaps, science fiction is providing foresight with its passion for authoritarianism; is this an example of an accurate prediction by SF authors? It would be nice if this were the case; unfortunately, I think that LeGuin had it right when she said that the authoritarian bent in science fiction has less to with visions of the future and more an "escape into the phoney…" An unreal world where leaders are always right, capitalism the only true economic system, and where the Galactic Fleet and the Galactic Chamber of Commerce rule the human dominated galaxy, and heroes never have to pay any taxes.

Unfortunately, if the present trends continue the phoney may become reality; the future is fascist.

---

[7] The early industrial period was powered by wind and water and thus factories were small-scale cottage industries. This part of the industrial period was more an evolution than a revolution; once the steam engine had been perfected to operate the factory machinery it became an Industrial Revolution.

[8] Of course candidates had to be politically acceptable (not socialist or communist) and racially acceptable (not Jewish, Slavic, Celtic, etc.) and be approved by the Interior Ministry – but, there were municipal elections; the only elections permitted under the Nazis.

Thrashing Trufen Archival Swill

Neil Jamieson-Williams

Just a few notes on the surviving Swill archive...

Archive Inventory:

Swill #1

- Mimeograph stencils wrapped in newspaper (Globe and Mail March 28, 1981)

- Remaindered (and quite smudged) mimeo copies of page 3 as well as about 25 copies of page 6 (the Maplecon Slandersheet)

- 20 copies of the Swill #1 -- at least that is what is written on the paper bag; in actuality there are close to thirty copies. It is also stated on the paper bag that this is the first edition and first print run; that is incorrect it is the second print run.

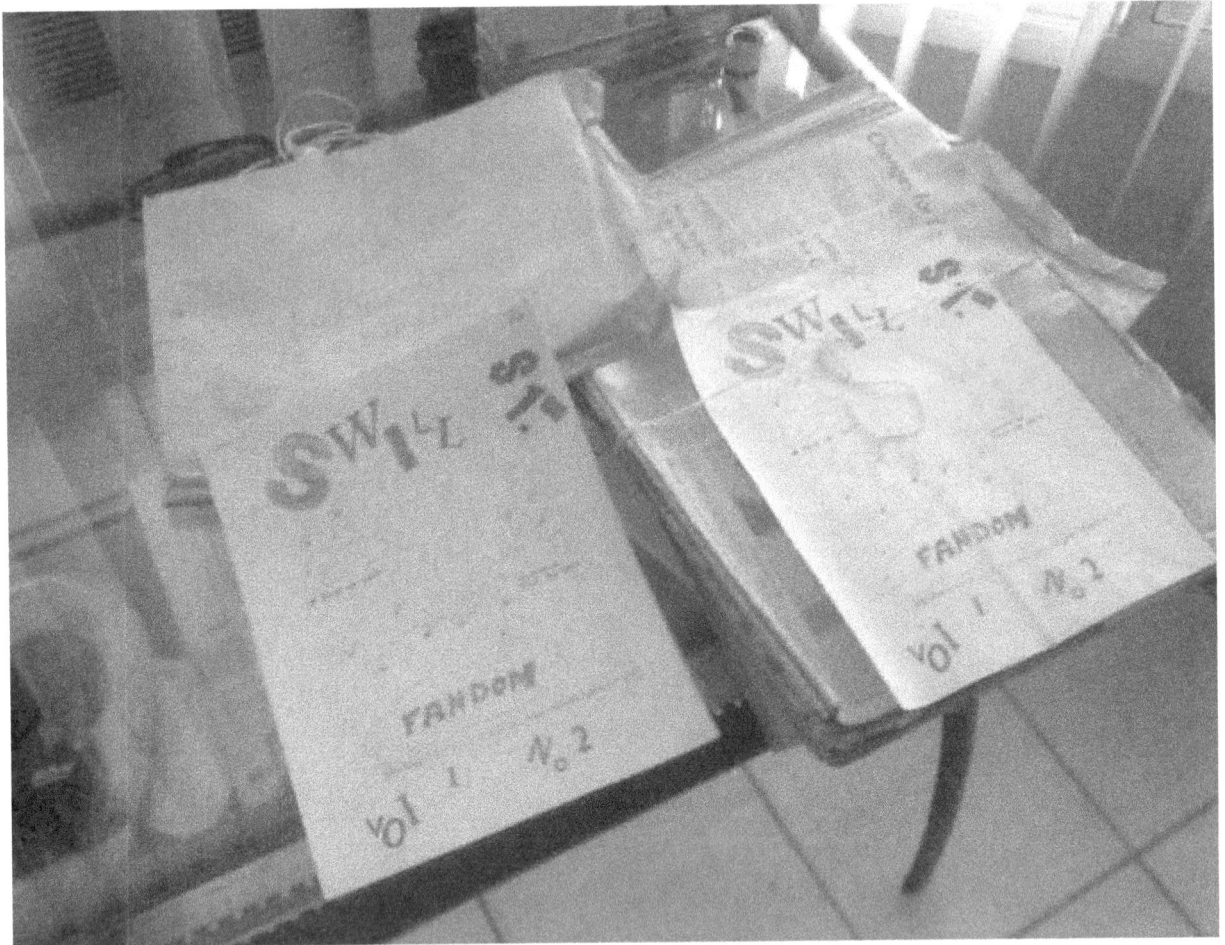

Swill #2

- Mimeograph stencils wrapped in newspaper (Globe and Mail March 28, 1981)

- 20 copies of the Swill #2 -- at least that is what is written on the paper bag; in actuality there are close to thirty copies. In this case the rest of what is written on the paper bag is correct, it is the first edition and first print run of this issue.

Other Stuff

- The 1976 issue of Reticulum; reproduced by ditto (spirit duplicator) and quite faded.

- Poem written by Jamieson-Williams; again in ditto and very faded.

- Issue #2 (and final issue) of Sirius Science Fiction, duplicated by ditto and very faded.

- Issue #1 of Sirius Science Fiction, printed via offset and a little yellowed.

Sirius Science Fiction #1 is the only document that could be scanned and converted into a pdf. However, I am not certain that I really want to do this. I have re-read the issue and to be blunt, my content really does suck, end of story. The only excuse (albeit lame) that I can give is that at the time that Sirius #1 was published I was 16 years of age; I would have turned 17 by the time issue #2 was published thus, the wise decision to cease further publication of the fanzine. Reticulum 1976 has no content of mine within it and although it may be possible to scan this as a pdf, I really have no legal rights to do so. The other two documents are far too faded and Sirius #2 is unreadable beyond the cover and table of contents.

Pissing on a Pile of Old Amazings:

...a modest column by Lester Rainsford

Elsewhere *The Swill* has commented on the sequels to Schmitx's _Witches of Karres_. It is true that I mentioned them to him but ther's another point coming too. For the most part, I agree with *The Swill's* criticisms.but it seems to me that they are like launching a torpedo to kill a goldfish, expensive overkill. No one expects thyat a couple of books wirtten by a various team of authors close to fifty years later will write something that is as good as the kind of originial that actually prompts sequels fifty years later. A not too unpleasant experience is the best we hope for. Personally, my biggest problem with the second, non-Lakcey book, was the amount of retelling and embellishing events that were barely mentioned in the original._Witches of Karres_ was an orignial, and stands pretty unique even in Schmitz work. I don't believe even Schmitz could write an appropriate sequel (though he did try apparently), and I sure don't expect it from a team of Baen writers.However, they *should* get more creative and come up with their own ideas rather than endlessly rehashing someone elses./

Given that Swill has been giving Fuck You to sf and fandom since 1980. And given that punk as I understand it is to do shitkicking to the old and dumb and basically lame. Could *The Swill's* lament that the Karres sequels don't match his reading of the original be.....antipunk? Waaah, sequels don't bring me back to my goldan age of sf waah waaaaah. Just the sort of pov that would be shitkicked by fuck you fandom all the way to Porlumma.

Ah but there is method to *The Swill's* work.This is a world where we get crappy prequels to entertaining films from olden days and now we are seeing a marketing blizz for the 3d *rerelease* of some crappy prequel to an entertaining film or two (yeah StarWars). Repackage and 'update' something that was good back then, and tell us that *tthese* are the good times, we're getting good stuff, as good as the originals, go out and consume, yay! We are getting sequels to Karres and bherbert has taken up dune and is giving us more more more.but somehow these aren't the good times.Shictckiciking them is the only answer really.

Yeah so much sf today is overwritten and endlessly elaborates itself to get a iokea-bookshelf-collapsing series out of a trivial event through more detail and pointless events than you can shake a broken ikea bookshelf at. Fuck you! Longing for the good old days of your own golden age and the good stuff from raheinlein and clarke and others? That's lame and should be shitkicked. The present sucks, not for quantity but for quality. Lester is a slow reader and reading endlessly detailed details about a hero that the author obviusly like s way more than Lester does makes Lester put down the book and refer to Lester in the third person.

HOWEVER. Going back to the golden age isnt the answer.. I have an ingenious proposal that unfortuantel is a little too long to be contained int he miserly column space allocated by *The Swil*

Flogging a Dead Trekkie: Classic Butchery

Neil Jamieson-Williams

The original title of this article was "When Some Swine Guts a Thing You Love", but I decided on this less emotional title instead. That doesn't mean that there will be no emotion; there will be and most of it in the form of anger. The subject of this article is a classic SF novel, The Witches of Karres written by James H. Schmitz. I do not have a favourite SF novel, I have a small constellation[9] of favourite novels and The Witches of Karres has been part of that constellation for longer than any of the other members. It is the closest I have to a favourite novel and it is one that I re-read at least once every three years.

Actually, it was Lester Rainsford who first clued me in on it being a novel. I had read the novella version that appeared in the book club edition of Science Fiction Hall of Fame, Volume 2 but had no idea that it had been expanded into a novel in 1966. It was also Lester who, at SFContario 2 last November, suggested that I read the sequels. I had heard of the sequels, I had read the backcover blubs in ChaptersIndigo, and a few professional reviews on the books; all together, this did not inspire me to want to go out and read these books. Since I knew Lester to have a liking for Schmitz's work, I followed his suggestion and did so. While the act of reading both The Wizard of Karres and The Sorceress of Karres did not require an extended visit to the vomitorium[10], it did have the effect of leaving one with the experience of consuming something that has almost, but not quite seriously, gone off. Hmm… that response is perhaps too cerebral. A more emotional and gut response would be that both sequels are absolute, pure unadulterated, chicken shit – in fact, faecal matter from diseased chickens.

The sad thing is that Schmitz actually did write a sequel himself, probably in the 1970's, titled "Karres Venture" that was lost in a house move. From there, we have two versions of the story

---

[9] Some of the other members of this cohort are: The Stars My Destination, Childhood's End, A Clockwork Orange, The Left Hand of Darkness, The Shores of Another Sea, The Gods Themselves, The World Menders, Bug Jack Baron, Rendezvous With Rama, The Dispossessed, Neuromancer, The End of the World News, Always Coming Home, A Fire Upon the Deep…

[10] Actually, a vomitorium is a series of entrance/exit passages in a Roman amphitheatre; I am using the term in its popular misconception form as a type of lavatory room used for the sole purpose of throwing up.

regarding the notes for the novel, perhaps both apocryphal. In one version, the notes were lost with the manuscript and in the other the notes survived, but nobody knows what became of them. Nevertheless, Schmitz never got around to re-writing the lost manuscript prior to his death in 1981.

Baen Books currently holds the rights (for those works not in public domain) to publish Schmitz works and Eric Flint has been assigned to edit these. I haven't taken the time to purchase the current Baen editions and then compare them to the earlier editions that I have, except for The Witches of Karres, and then not in a very thorough manner. I did do some comparison between my Ace edition[11] from the mid-1970's and the Baen edition; some of the old typos were gone but there are some new typos too. While this does not appear to be the case with the present Baen edition of The Witches of Karres (Flint's editing here is no more than copyediting and doesn't deserve the "edited by" credit on the front cover), I have heard from Schmitz fans that Flint has edited with a heavy hand some of Schmitz's other works. Where I am going here is that one would speculate, with some degree of confidence, that Mr. Flint would – with all this editing – have familiarity with the voice, the atmosphere, and the plot structure of a Schmitz novel. This would be a reasonable and logical assumption. Well, you know what they say about assumptions…

Based upon The Wizard of Karres and The Sorceress of Karres Flint does not have a strong familiarity with the works of James H. Schmitz. Ah, but maybe I am being a little unkind; these sequels are group projects, so other than a little bit of copyediting by Flint, I still have no firm data on how well he has edited other Schmitz material. I can however comment upon how competent Flint and friends are in creating new fiction in a Schmitz universe in a Schmitz style. The short answer; they are bloody fucking incompetent.

Where do I start? Do I begin with voice, or with atmosphere, or with plot? I will begin with voice as the cover blurbs for both sequels crow about how seamlessly F&F (Flint and Fiends) have recreated the writing style of Schmitz. This is complete rubbish. I will agree that the F&F writing collective have manufactured a style that does at times appear to be similar to or to bear a likeness to that of Schmitz, but it is not sustainable. It comes across as somebody pretending to be Schmitz and not doing a very good job of it. At best, they can sort of resemble the writing style of Schmitz, and perhaps they could even sustain this resemblance, if they didn't resort to cheap tricks that immediately disintegrate their construct. Cheap tricks? How about mining the

---

[11] This was easy as I had marked up the old Ace edition noting the typos in it. I did this because back in the late 1990's the book had been out of print for years and I was attempting to buy the publication rights for it from the current rights holder, Baen Books; who, at the time had no intention of selling the rights and no intention of ever publishing the novel again (sort of like a dragon with its hoard of gold).

original for what could be termed "quotable phrases" – phrases usually only used once in the entire novel – that are now rebranded by F&F as catch-phrases and cliches that they pepper throughout the two sequels. Another failure point is in place names. Schmitz place names tend to sound real, and for a good reason; sometimes they are actual real place names and other times Schmitz has anglicised those real place names in his own unique personal way.[12] Now, I have no idea as to what Schmitz would create as a name for a circus planet, should he ever have had the need to create one, but I can tell you that it would be, somehow, based upon a real place name; it would never be a moronic and complete fabrication such as Vaudevillia. The voice created by the F&F writers group project is inauthentic and false. It is as if they weren't really actually trying. And yet, one would expect that Flint should know better, but there is no evidence of that.

One would also expect Flint, at least, to be familiar with the atmosphere of a Schmitz novel and, in particular, the atmosphere of the Karres universe. Once again, this expectation is not met by F&F. It is as if the writing collective had not actually read the original novel; one could speculate that F&F were provided with a Coles Notes[13] plot summary of The Witches of Karres by editorial and given carte blanche to do whatever they wanted to with the material provided they produce a sequel manuscript in 90 days. It certainly does appear that F&F did not put in a lot of effort into writing their sequels as the atmosphere that Schmitz had created is not only absent, it has been rendered into a comic book greaves.

The atmosphere of Schmtz's Karres universe has a mild sense of mystery in a sense of there being the unknown. Much of this sense of the unknown is created through classic Schmitz understatement. Humans have been out among the stars for thousands of years – how many thousands is not stated – long enough that the location of our homeworld is never mentioned and simply referred to as Old Yarthe[14]. We are informed several things about the past in general; that there are ancient[15] legends of the Great Eastern Wars, that the Far Galactic East is unknown, that the Empire has, in centuries past, been at times larger and at other times smaller than it is today, and that in recent centuries the world of Uldune had been the centre of a pirate confederacy that challenged even the military might of the Empire. Schmitz doesn't give actual dates, only vague relative dates which serves to create a setting that contains both the known and unknown, as well as mystery. While the original novel takes place predominantly within the sections of the galaxy inhabited by humans, there is also the implication that the human "sphere of influence" is just

---

[12] Karres is an actual village in Austria. Nikeldepain, Emris, Uldune, and Chaladoor are all the product of minor Schmitz-morphing of the spelling of real place names in the Netherlands, Wales, the Middle East, and Indonesia.
[13] Those readers from the US will be more familiar with the term CliffsNotes. Coles Notes were first published by the Coles bookchain in Canada in 1948 which licensed the US rights to Cliff Hillegass in 1958.
[14] In indication of linguistic drift over the millennia.
[15] The distant past, minimum 1,500 years ago.

one small part of the galactic whole. Entering into Schmitz's Karres universe invokes and atmosphere similar to entering into a European inn that has existed continuously, in one form or another, as a hostelry for over a millennium; there is a sense of age and feeling of history about the place.

Of course, all of that atmosphere evaporates before a supernova wavefront when a pack of toad-brained troglodytes – in this case the F&F group project – make one single statement in their sequels; the Empire is a human-centric galactic empire, a la Star Wars. With one simple statement F&F vent much of the atmosphere of the Karres universe and trivialise it into a cartoon-like tourist attraction or theme park.

Some of the remaining atmosphere is eroded away when, for no purpose, F&F make changes to Karres universe starship propulsion systems. Schmitz, like many SF authors of his time period assumed that in the future spaceships would be propelled by some form of antigravity or reaction less (or apparently reaction less) space drive; rockets were just the most primitive way to get into space. While some authors gave their drives names (usually after their inventor) and others also provided some sort of explanation as to how the drive works; Schmitz does neither, period. The drives require fuel (unspecified) that supplies them with power (unspecified) so that they can propel the ship at different velocities using different drives. *Venture 7333* has a main drive, used in interstellar travel, which can be also be placed into overdrive. The secondary drives appear to be used for atmospheric and interplanetary travel and can, if necessary, be used for interstellar travel at velocities implied (but never stated) to be only a few times that of the speed of light. The underdrives are used in landing and take-off. A good take-off is described as a ship "...floating into space, as sedately as a swan..." This is so definitely describing some form of antigravity or spacedrive that the word obvious would be appropriate.

And yet, for some reason, this is not obvious to F&F; perhaps this is because nobody in the group project thought it was necessary to actually read The Witches of Karres, or if they did read the book, to take any notes. In their australopithecine wisdom F&F have decided that the underdrives and the secondary drives are powered by some form of rocket? Why is this so? Beats me. I cannot think of a rational or logical or intelligent reason for making this change. According to one professional reviewer this was a great plot device. Uh; no, it is not. Any plot tension that arises from placing Venture and her crew in the position of running out of fuel and/or not being able to afford to purchase fuel[16] does not automatically result in the ship being

---

[16] Actually a less desperate version of this plot device is used in the original novella; Pausert has used up too much fuel during a prolonged run in overdrive and has to refuel at exorbitant prices.

powered by rockets. Again, this is further deterioration of atmosphere in the Karres universe has no purpose; other than to cheapen the universe itself.

Then there is plot... I don't get what went on here on the part of Flint, et al; especially as Flint supposedly has edited all of Schmitz's work published by Baen – one would expect him to be familiar with the standard Schmitz plot structure. Yes indeed, Schmitz could be formulaic, but he had a very interesting formula that he tended to use in a unique manner. The standard Schmitz plot goes like this: the protagonist has a problem that they believe that they have resolved or almost resolved; it is a problem that is minor and personal, only affecting the protagonist and those closest to them. Either the resolution of the original problem or a decision made now adds to the original problem or hands the protagonist a larger problem. This process continues until the protagonist is now facing a world-changing, fate of millions/the world/humankind problem at the climax of the novel that they have to resolve – and sometimes the Schmitz protagonist only partial resolves the problem, i.e. removing the immediate threat to all but the problem yet remains; usually because it is something that can only be resolved by a large group of people or society itself, not a single protagonist and their cohorts. Neither of these sequels has an authentic Schmitz plotline; they have fairly standard, space opera, adventure plots, but they do not have Schmitz plots.

F&F remind me of Dexter from the first season. In the first season of the television series, once Dexter (a serial killer who hunts other serial killers) had taken his blood slide trophy from his victim, he would then proceed to carve them up, initially while still alive with his circular saw and/or other cutting tools. F&F have taken the still living and breathing body that is The Witches of Karres (which unlike Dexter's victims is an innocent) and placed it on their table so that they can vivisect for their masters; who own the rights to this "property". These literary ghouls carve out pieces of dialogue, character, and numerous plot threads and fragments from the source text, which they combine with some chunks they have carved out of other victims, that they then use to cobble together their Shelley-esque golems. Without respect and with great abandon, F&F have eviscerated a much loved classic. The products of this butchery are the two Baen sequels.

Fortunately, this analogy, while it describes the process with great precision, is imprecise in regards to the end result. Unlike Dexter's victims, The Witches of Karres is potentially immortal. F&F can carve chunks out of the original novel and use these pieces to construct their patchwork sequels; but they cannot harm it. The Witches of Karres is a well-loved classic – the sequels just tawdry, tinsel, throw-away commodities that will be forgotten with the passage of time.

Scribbling on the Bog Wall:
Letters of Comment

Neil Jamieson-Williams

As I write this, there is only two LoCs this time around. As always, my comments are in red.

Subject: Re: Your latest Swill is now available
From: "Taral Wayne" <Taral@teksavvy.com>
Date: Tue, January 17, 2012 6:37 pm
To: swill@uldunemedia.ca
Priority: Normal
Options: View Full Header | View Printable Version | Download this as a file

Pissmonkey is bad enough, but in red my eyes watered. Fortunately, the .pdf was a little clearer than your site (for some reason) and could be blown up as well. After that, it wasn't so bad. It still seems to me to be an ill-advised idea to deliberatly lay obstacles in the path of your readers, and it doesn't seem like good academia, either. Then again, maybe it is... When has academia ever wanted to be understood by the lay reader?

Academia is a sort of a "trufandom" in its in-groupishness, wouldn't you say?

Subject: Re: Your latest Swill is now available
From: swill@uldunemedia.ca
Date: Wed, January 18, 2012 12:12 pm
To: "Taral Wayne" <Taral@teksavvy.com>
Priority: Normal
Options: View Full Header | View Printable Version | Download this as a file

Hi Taral,

You are correct that pudmonkey is clearer in pdf than in html (plus you can blow it up -- I prefer somewher between 125 and 150%).

As for continued use of the font... FYI, I have been using it for Swill related stuff since 2001; the Tripod site was originally all in pudmonkey. So, it has sort of become a new Swill tradition. Perhaps, the difficult font is an obstacle for the reader, but, I also like the font and find it aesthetically pleasing a a grunge sort of manner. Yes, I do realise that I am electing form over function. I will however consider one change, next issue I will (probably) not place my comments in red bolded pudmonkey.

The pudmonkey choice is one based on style and image and has nothing to do with academe. Academics often want to be understood by the lay reader, though this is a problem of juggling audiences as well as career advancement. Writing a academic book that is printed by a peer-reviewed publisher counts more for career advancement than a book written for a general audience. With limited time, academics will tend to put more effort into writing peer-reviewed books, which serve to increase their academic status (and salary) than they would to write books that popularise the subject material. It is still slightly frowned upon and usually does not count as an academic publication. Now, if your popular book is made into a BBC or PBS documentary series, you will score brownie points -- not with your fellow academics -- but with your college/university administrators which can be good for your career.

Also, many academics are not able to write for a general audience but only for their own peers -- usually this also means that they are poor teachers at the undergraduate level but excellent at the graduate level. Sometimes we will write a hybrid book that contains material that is accessible to the interested layperson while also possessing the rigour of the academic's discipline. This is not an easy task; I have tried it and been only partially successful at it -- usually both your general readers and your academic readers are left unsatisfied. I'll be trying this again this year and will let your know how that goes...

Academe is indeed full of in-groupness and "trufan" definitions; e.g. in sociology your choice of research methodology and your theoretical paradigm will place you within certain "trufan" groups and designate you as a "fakefan" in the eyes of others. However, these games are not over ephemeral status as in fandom but on real status that can effect reputation and career and salary.

All the best,
Neil

Subject: Re: Your latest Swill is now available
From: "Taral Wayne" <Taral@teksavvy.com>
Date: Wed, January 18, 2012 3:15 pm
To: swill@uldunemedia.ca
Priority: Normal
Options: View Full Header | View Printable Version | Download this as a file

I can almost see replacing "academic" with "priest" and "academia" with "the Church" and the whole thing still working... But I understand. Pulling legs and tweaking noses is also fannish tradition... as long as no sharp implements are involved.

And there are harder things to read.

That comparison has been made before; it has some validity, but only some. It is an inexact comparison.

I agree that there are harder things to read. Much, much harder. No I am the first to admit that my penmanship is not very good, it is actually bad and I recall the pointer swats that were supposed to condition me toward better penmanship. That said, the general standard of penmanship has declined over the years. You think that the pudmonkey font is hard to read, try reading 120 plus pencil-scrawled essay question exams; pudmonkey will be a welcome relief after that.

Nevertheless, read further in the letters column to receive thy reward...

1706-24 Eva Rd.
Etobicoke, ON
M9C 2B2

February 14, 2012

Dear Neil:

I have been dragging my ass when it comes to writing letters, but I am starting to get moving again. I have here issue 11 of Swill @ 30.

First of all, in talking to John Purcell, I find I must apologize to you. When I reviewed Swill @ 30 in my fanzine review column a while ago now, I thought I had all my facts straight. My training is in journalism. But it looks like I didn't, and I wouldn't have written what I did if I didn't think it was correct. My apologies, and in talking with John, he said he's giving you the opportunity to set the record straight, and explain Swill to a larger audience. You do say in the first paragraph that memory is neither as clear nor as correct as we often think it is...I may have just proved it.

Hi Lloyd,
No sweat, really. Nor any offence. I just want to make sure the correct information is out there... I don't mind being thrashed in print for something I actually did or said, but it is a pain when it happens over something that you didn't say or do or information that is wrong.

I don't have any problems with the Pudmonkey font...the real function of the font is to concentrate your focus beyond the relative illegibility of it, and concentrate on what's been written.

Read on...there are changes afoot.

Trufen...I have read a lot about the history of fandom, and so many of us hold our fannish forefathers in high regard. Today, some people I won't name seem to push themselves up by pushing others down. Trufen, trufandom...it is an excuse to be exclusive and snobbish. Such as it's always been, I gather, and such as it is in many other activities and hobbies. We're nothing new, and frankly, others do it better. Being inclusive and trying my best to accept new people and new interests are the main reasons why Yvonne and I have been around fandom, for all its good and bad, for about 35 years.

Yes, I will get back on this track in issue #13 (I promise this time). I personally prefer to be inclusive, up to a point; I will defer to expertise and become exclusive if the task at hand requires it. Unless you are talking about negotiating a hotel contract, or how to properly run the various AV devices, or how to design a really high end website (and these skills are not ones exclusive to fandom) there is no real fan expertise. There are those that know local fan history, those who know the complete list of all local conventions and the GoHs going back to the very first con in 194x, etc. Wonderful. And when I was head of shipping-receiving I had order-pickers who knew could identify any vehicle, tell you the year it was introduced, what came standard, etc. They were not snobbish or exclusive about this knowledge, self appointed trufen are.

Good to be able to make corrections on the record of past issues. SFContario 2 was fun, and we were on a variety of panels. Looks like voicework may be a future aspect of the convention's programming, and seeing I've done some, I'll have another way to have some fun.

SFContario was fun, I look forward to attending it again this year.

Poor Fritz? We saw the tolchocking Fritz got on a regular basis, and we laughed, but still, after years of that, poor Fritz! True, steampunk costuming will be done in some years, but in the meantime, we're having some fun. Our own costuming activities go back to the 80s. We know of some folks who have left the steampunk group, and are looking for something new to see and do, so there's the first sign that it may be close to jumping the shark.

Steampunk costuming won't disappear; it will just cease to be something everybody does. I think that it is an interesting sub-genre though I agree with Lester that sometimes things are not very well thought through – the science in the science fiction is often lacking and just gadgetry.

Done for now, I think...we wound up not going to Futurecon. We had paid for everything in advance, but money became so tight, we decided to ask for it back, and it paid some late bills. Things are a little better now, and we are starting to plan for Ad Astra. Looks like we'll see you there.

Yours, Lloyd Penney.

See you at Ad Astra…

BCSFAzine 464 Review of Swill @ 30 #9

Neil uses my mention of Swill in my review of Graeme's Auroran Lights as a "LOC." I approve of this technique, since I'm too lazy to write both a review of and a LOC to any given zine....It sounds like the original

Swill was a cross between the punk attitude of the time and the present-day Internet trolls. This thought occurs to me partly because in the last few days I've wondered if I should invent nerd-punk.

Font criticism: As has been noted by other Swill @ 30 readers, the Pudmonkey font is hard to read. However, I can go a step further and recommend a more read - able font that should still achieve the desired effect: VTCorona.

Felicity, thank you for your input. Note to comrades Taral and the Graeme; one gets much further by making a criticism and then offering an alternative that one does by simply bitching and whining.

As of Issue #13, the pudmonkey font will be used for column/article titles and contributor names and VT Corona shall be used for content. For an example, see Endnote.

Endnote: Good Old Days

Neil Jamieson-Williams

In the Good Old Days... The hearing of this phrase should give
one a chill as the utterance of it is usually the introduction to
a monologue that one is about to receive concerning the flaws of
any generation or age set younger than that of the person doing
the uttering. In brief, the speaker will extol the virtues of
another time, when all things were wonderful, during some form of
golden age that has for ever gone. Often there is the additional
jab that younger generations are too benighted to understand what
has been lost and they are also one of the reasons why such a
former utopian period will never come again. And typical
nostalgic rubbish like that.

As is stated very well in the recent film, <u>Midnight in Paris</u>,
golden ages are at best, very subjective. Two individuals from
the same age set may have very different perceptions as to when
the "golden age" was and, if one could go back in time to your
particular "golden age" there would be people from that time
period who long for a different time in the past. That is the
tthing with "golden ages"; they all exist in the past.

I do not suffer from any strong melancholic desire to reside in
another period in history; though, a holiday would be interesting
(so long as one had all their shots and took other precautions).
Of course, causality probably prevents this from ever being a
possibility. There is no period in my own life that I wish I
could just chuck everything and return to -- again, there are
some periods that would be cool to visit briefly (even if one
could only visit via a recording device). But again, this is no
burning desire. While I do have some nostalgia for particular
books that I have read and re-read over the years -- I have no

interest in only reading old books[17]. There are no "good old days" when all was right with the world.

I have poked my head back into fandom for a year now. All I can say is that some things are much the same as they were thirty years ago and some things are not; almost all of these changes have to do changes that have occurred in the larger (mainstream) culture and impacted upon the SF fan subculture. I have no desire to go back to Toronto fandom of the late 1970's or Vancouver fandom of the 1980's. Those who do long for their subjective, fannish, golden age are free to do so; it is their own personal choice[18] to make. I may not think it is a wise choice. I may think it is an exclusive choice. But otherwise, I really don't care. Except, should they take it the next step and cloak their version of a golden age as being synonymous with trufan membership; then, they become pain-in-the-ass shitheads that I personally don't want anything to do with[19]. And should they launch into one of their in-the-good-old-days monologues; it is time to move somewhere far, far away.

---

[17] Likewise for music, a lot of the music on my iPod is from the 1980's and early 1990's, but there is a large segment that are much more recent; as well, there is some flux, there is what is on my iPod and what is on my playlist -- artists like Nick Cave and Crass are on my iPod but not on my playlist.
[18] I am old enough to know people who, based on their music collections, are of the firm opinion that no new music has been recorded since 1979.
[19] Though they do make good research informants, aka subjects.

Original image determined to be too dark and would
create bleed-through ((

Original image was a defacement of the
Potlach 21 convention poster

CODA

A list of SWILL volumes:

Original SWILL	issues 1 through 7
SWILL 2011	issues 8 through 12
SWILL 2012	issues 13 through 17
SWILL 2013	issues 18 through 22
SWILL 2014	issues 23 through 26
SWILL 2015	issues 27 through 30
SWILL 2016/2017	issues 31 through 35
SWILL Annuals: Volume 1	issues 36 through 40

Vile Fen Press

a division of Klatha Entertainment an Uldune Media company

www.ingramcontent.com/pod-product-compliance
Lightning Source LLC
Chambersburg PA
CBHW081256040426
42452CB00014B/2523